"You'll be challenged to become a better kind of leader—a different, spiritually potent kind of leader. Nelson sums it up well: 'Spiritual leaders must be spiritual first, leaders second.'"
—Thom and Joani Schultz, chief officers, Group Publishing; authors of *The Dirt on Learning*

"Dr. Alan Nelson has crafted another helpful book, *Spirituality and Leadership*. His lucid style shines and his content is worthy. I commend this book with enthusiasm."
—Leslie Parrot, Ph.D., president emeritus, Olivet Nazarene University

"Alan Nelson raises the penetrating questions all leaders need to ask of their souls. Finally we have a leadership resource that challenges us to think far beyond what we do to who we really are."
—Gene Appel, senior pastor, Central Christian Church, Henderson, Nevada

"Alan Nelson's book on spirituality and leadership will challenge, stretch, and question some of your premises in both spirituality and leadership. If you think you know everything about leadership and spirituality, you don't until you read this book."
—Elmer L. Towns, dean, School of Religion, Liberty University, Lynchburg, Virginia

"Alan Nelson has written a long overdue book on the issue of spiritual leadership. With the strong, obvious interest in spirituality in today's society, he has hit a home run with his candid, in-depth look at the path to spiritual leadership. Any leader desiring to discover value and identity in Christ will benefit from this book. I plan to give a copy to all of my church leaders."
—Stan Toler, author, pastor, Oklahoma City, Oklahoma

"Finally! In a culture that has settled for one-dimensional leadership, this inspired book guides us beyond the overworked and into the unexplored. *Spirituality and Leadership* is a vital tool for developing spiritual leaders on every level of life. Read it and grow your soul!"

—Terry M. Crist, pastor, CitiChurch International; author of *Learning the Language of Babylon* and *Awakened to Destiny*

"*Spirituality and Leadership* is a brave attempt to mix the nitrogen of leadership and the glycerin of spirituality in a way that creates a powerful and much needed synergy of two previously uncombined subjects."

—Brad Smith, Leadership Network

"I just finished teaching my 17th doctoral course on leadership. Unfortunately, I did not have his book on the reading list. It will be on the next."

—Dr. John Vawter, former president, Phoenix Seminary; senior pastor, Bethany Community Church; director of *You're Not Alone*

"Alan has addressed the most critical need for the 21st century church: spiritual leadership."

—Mike Slaughter, author of *unLearning Church*

"I love the questions this book asks. And in his answers, Alan Nelson never becomes overly mystical or mechanical. He helps us all be stronger, spiritually growing leaders."

—Kevin Miller, vice president, Christianity Today International

HARNESSING THE WISDOM, GUIDANCE, AND POWER OF THE SOUL

Spirituality&Leadership

ALAN E. NELSON

NAVPRESS

Bringing Truth to Life
P.O. Box 35001, Colorado Springs, Colorado 80935

OUR GUARANTEE TO YOU

We believe so strongly in the message of our books that we are making this quality guarantee to you. If for any reason you are disappointed with the content of this book, return the title page to us with your name and address and we will refund to you the list price of the book. To help us serve you better, please briefly describe why you were disappointed. Mail your refund request to: NavPress, P.O. Box 35002, Colorado Springs, CO 80935.

The Navigators is an international Christian organization. Our mission is to reach, disciple, and equip people to know Christ and to make Him known through successive generations. We envision multitudes of diverse people in the United States and every other nation who have a passionate love for Christ, live a lifestyle of sharing Christ's love, and multiply spiritual laborers among those without Christ.

NavPress is the publishing ministry of The Navigators. NavPress publications help believers learn biblical truth and apply what they learn to their lives and ministries. Our mission is to stimulate spiritual formation among our readers.

Library of Congress Catalog Card Number: 2002002128
ISBN 1-57683-260-0

Cover design by Dan Jamison
Cover illustration by Greg Hargreaves / Artville
Creative Team: Brad Lewis, Amy Spencer, Glynese Northam

Some of the anecdotal illustrations in this book are true to life and are included with the permission of the persons involved. All other illustrations are composites of real situations, and any resemblance to people living or dead is coincidental.

Unless otherwise identified, all Scripture quotations in this publication are taken from the *HOLY BIBLE: NEW INTERNATIONAL VERSION*® (NIV®). Copyright © 1973, 1978, 1984 by International Bible Society. Used by permission of Zondervan Publishing House. All rights reserved.

Nelson, Alan E.
  Spirituality and leadership : harnessing the wisdom, guidance, and power of the soul / Alan E. Nelson.
    p. cm.
Includes bibliographical references.
  ISBN 1-57683-260-0
  1. Clergy--Office. 2. Clergy--Religious life. 3. Christian leadership. 4. Pastoral theology. I. Title.
BV660.3 .N45 2002
  253--dc21   2002002128

Printed in the United States of America

1 2 3 4 5 6 7 8 9 10 / 06 05 04 03 02

Contents

How Do Spiritual Leaders Create a Culture That
  Nurtures the Soul?
What Do Relationships in an Organization Have to
  Do with Spiritual Leadership?
What Are Some Indicators of Spiritual Leading Found
  in Relationships and Attitudes?
What Happens When a Spiritual Leader Fails?
What Happens When the Goal or the Organization
  Fails?

Foreword

For Such Times as These

A shipwrecked mariner had spent several years on a deserted island. Then one morning he couldn't believe his eyes. There was a ship offshore and a smaller vessel pulling out toward him.

When the boat grounded on the beach, the officer in charge handed the marooned sailor a bundle of newspapers. "With the captain's compliments," he said. "The captain wants you to read through these and let us know if you still want to be rescued."

We are living in wacko times. And the times are getting wackier. There's a lot about these postmodern "times" that I don't like or understand.

As a writer, I don't like it that I'm living in a world where "the most powerful character in modern melodrama" is a cannibal and psychopath named Hannibal Lecter.[1]

As an academic, trained in a Gutenberg curriculum and context, I don't like it that films influence my kids more than books do.

As a professor at a university and a resident of Washington State, it is somewhat mortifying to learn that there is now at Washington State University a Taco Bell Distinguished Professor of Hotel and Restaurant Administration[2] (how can somebody holding a Taco Bell Chair be distinguished, I want to know?). There is now at Stanford University (no slouch school) a Yahoo! Chair with an emphasis on information systems technology.[3] The most "distinguished" professors of marketing at the universities of Arizona and West Virginia hold the Coca Cola Chair and the K-Mart Chair respectively.[4]

As a father, I am horrified that TV's so-called "family hour" is filled with explicit sexual material and jokes about oral sex, masturbation, pornography, and homosexuality. During Fox's family hour,

Boston Public actually showed teenagers in a school hallway engaging in oral sex.[5] I am angered by some of the images and antics of MTV.

As a USAmerican, I am embarrassed by what Read Mercer Schuchardt calls the "complete cultural victory of pornography in America today." Hollywood releases four hundred films each year. The $10-billion-a-year pornography industry releases seven hundred movies each month. The domain name "business.com" recently sold for a record-breaking $7.5 million. The domain name "sex.com" is valued at $65 million.[6]

As a human being, I am scandalized by the fact that postmoderns are more likely to be outraged by the suggestion of violence to animals than they are by the slaughter of their own kind. I've been to movies where, in the process of making the movie, actors and stunt crew were injured, maimed, or killed, yet there was the assurance at the end of the credits that "no animals have been harmed during the production of this movie." In one movie about insects, they even said "no insects were killed during the production of this movie."

This is not the time I would have picked. But God has picked us for such times as these. That's why we need this book. Alan Nelson opens up a rich and exciting world linking spirituality and leadership, one that still largely awaits discovery in the church. Nelson's understanding of spirituality focuses less on spiritual moments than on a momentous spirituality. And his understanding of leadership is more biblically informed than culturally fashioned. In short, this is a study that brings together the two most requisite topics for such times as these.

Very early in the movie *The Lord of the Rings* (2002), Frodo says he wishes the master ring had not been found in his lifetime. "So do I," said Gandalf, "and so do all who live to see such times. But that is not for them to decide. All we have to decide is what to do with the time that is given us."

No matter how bizarre or off-putting the times given us, spiritual leaders are those who will "be there."

—LEONARD SWEET
Drew University
George Fox University
preachingplus.com

A Call for Spiritual Leadership

Why do we need spiritual leaders?

What does a spiritual leader look like?

Why is spiritual leading needed in the twenty-first century?

What do we mean by the terms "spiritual," "leadership," and "spiritual leadership"?

Tucked away in Prescott, Arizona, is a quaint coffee shop in St. Michael's Hotel, one of my favorite writing spots. The view from the window tables is an old-fashioned town square with a county courthouse, right out of the movie *Back to the Future*. Actually, it's the city square where they filmed the fight scene from *Billy Jack*.

The coffee shop is at the corner of Gurley and Montezuma streets. At this corner is the only place in Prescott—perhaps in the world—where you can be on both Gurley and Montezuma streets at the same time. Like the crossing point of many other streets in the world, this forty-by-forty-foot section of pavement is called an intersection.

Just like the unique intersections where two streets meet, this book is not only about spirituality or only about leadership. You might say it is about "soully" leading. Our goal is to study the intersection of spirituality and leadership, the exact spot where these two powerful concepts overlap.

Spiritual leadership is the focal point and the power plant for twenty-first-century leadership. In the past, we've looked to leaders (regardless of their spiritualities) to learn how to lead better. For spirituality, we've looked to desert fathers, enlightened gurus, pastors, and priests who were often clueless about leading.

Any elementary-school child can tell you that when you mix yellow paint with blue paint, the resulting color is green. To understand spiritual leadership, we can't merely study leadership and then study spirituality, assuming that the two different elements will naturally combine. Spiritual leadership has a color of its own. The characteristics of spiritual leadership are at times significantly different from the two individual elements.

If you don't understand both spirituality and leadership and how they interact, you'll be far less competent at leading in the coming years. Cutting-edge technology, product positioning, and market innovations fade in comparison to what will make twenty-first-century groups prevail. Dynamic organizations know that their strongest assets and liabilities are people. Individuals who unleash the synergy among people are called leaders.

The number of books on leadership is exploding. There is also a burgeoning interest in spirituality, reflected in the growing number of books on that topic. But it's the combination of these two fields that provides many solutions for a society hungry for a more evolved vision and governance.

These are ancient-future times. Our metamorphosis has taken us ahead to the past—or is it back to the future? We've transcended the age when people debunked God and the spiritual realm because they couldn't quantify them in a laboratory. We've tried science and found it wanting. While we've not thrown out the intellectual pursuit of truth and logic, we have transcended it. Like Goldilocks, we found the bed of religion too soft, the bed of technology too hard, and now we seek something just right. We've come to the realization that truth exists beyond the parameters of the explainable, observable, and at times, even the thinkable. Because effective leaders are social artists, they're both adapters to environmental influences and culture sculptors. The search for authentic spiritual leaders will grow as the twenty-first century dawns with mysteries and complexities none of us have yet experienced.

WHY DO WE NEED SPIRITUAL LEADERS?

What happens when you get hungry? Your stomach begins to gurgle and rumble. Well, here at the start of the twenty-first century, our culture is growling for spiritual leaders—men and women who understand both spirituality and leadership.

Our society seems to be crying out for people with both dominant characteristics. Leaders of the past sometimes dabbled in spiritual and religious activities, either for their private benefit or to be perceived as moral by others. But politically correct religiosity will not cut it in the high-demand world of the twenty-first century.

Have you ever read about advanced breeds of rats, insects, and bacteria that are immune to yesterday's poisons and vaccines? More subtle and powerful extermination techniques and inoculations must be developed or we'll be overrun by these enemies. Similarly, today's social and organizational ills resist yesterday's best practices. Most have evolved beyond simpler times when changes were few and far between. The complexities of twenty-first-century organizations mean previous leadership solutions don't work.

You can see the challenge of leading in the high turnover among corporate CEOs and the plethora of leadership books on the market as people grope for solutions. Savvy followers and collaborators require that those who lead them now and into the future have more skills than ever before. Leaders will need to go beyond their minds and lead from the wisdom, guidance, and power that comes from the soul. People yearn for those who will lead with head and heart and who will recognize the spiritual side of the people they lead.

What Does a Spiritual Leader Look Like?

One commonly model is a Hollywood science-fiction character: Obi-Wan Kenobi, the mentor in the *Star Wars* film series. Obi-Wan was a Jedi knight, a talented, intelligent, sage fighter for good. He was confident, but had no room for bravado. Instead, he relied upon the Force, an energy field that transcends all life forms.

Obi-Wan wasn't the traditional white male, riding into town on his steed, barking commands for naïve followers to obey. He was quietly humble yet competent. Experience had shown him that the world didn't revolve around him. But he also knew the importance of what he was called to do. Obi-Wan mentored a protégé, teaching him about the ways of the Force, not relying on technology or techniques alone. He ultimately sacrificed his life for the good of the cause, thus dying as he lived—for something bigger than himself.

One weakness of the Obi-Wan character was that he was disconnected from people, living alone in the desert. Prophetic types may appear to be leaders as they propose radical visions and often sacrifice their reputations and lives. But true leaders organize people toward causes. The regurgitation of a call to change is usually easier than the strong, subtle selling required by leaders who strive to implement change. Desert hermits are not leader types. While healthy leaders seem to detach themselves from the organization they serve, they remain in the thick of relationships. Twenty-first-century leadership is complex; teams of people are needed rather than a few talented individuals working on their own. Leaders must possess superior people skills, aligning their strengths with organizational needs.

Another shortcoming of Obi-Wan Kenobi as an effective model of spiritual leadership is that his spirituality seems to be without boundaries. You may remember that the Force was poorly defined and broadly vague. Of course, the film wasn't intended as a spiritual guide, but it does reveal much of what is wrong with today's popular version of spirituality. When spirituality is overly mystical and esoteric, it loses its impact. A faceless, wishy-washy energy field with no absolutes does little to help us focus on what is meaningful. Spirituality without boundaries tends to be diluted and powerless. Have you ever had a conversation with a person who appeared to be spiritual but had few definitions or guidelines for communicating it? If so, you know the difficulty in a homemade recipe for spiritual growth.

In this book, I'll define spirituality within the boundaries of classic Christian beliefs. Christianity has proven to be a powerful belief system over the years, centering on the life of Jesus. While many contemporary and historic groups have justified their selfish actions (such as "holy" wars and hate crimes) and attitudes with the Bible, these groups don't represent classic Christianity. Rogue associates—people who are out of line with stated values—exist in every group. But does every employee in your company adequately represent the organization all the time? No. And not every action done in the name of Christ represents the truth of Christianity.

However, the timelessness of the Bible's teachings provides enduring boundaries for us to define spirituality.

WHY IS SPIRITUAL LEADING NEEDED IN THE TWENTY-FIRST CENTURY?

One of my hobbies is collecting leadership books, posters, and symbols. Curiously, a number of these items feature eagles. The eagle may have once been an acceptable symbol of leaders. But I don't think it's valid for this century. Eagles tend to be loners. They don't lead flocks. They basically look out for themselves—picking out weak prey and living high above everything.

A better leadership analogy for the twenty-first century is the game of chess. In this analogy, a leader is both the player and a chess piece. Chess consists of a team of pieces, each with different strengths and weaknesses: pawns, rooks, bishops, knights, a queen and king. Each has value to the team and a different movement pattern. Ironically, the king, the key to winning or losing the game, is as vulnerable as a pawn and can even be weaker. But the goal of the entire team is to capture the opponent's king.

In the game of chess, as in life, the playing field is complex and changing. When the opponent moves a single chess piece, multiple threats and opportunities arise from the action. You can think ahead, but you'll likely have to change your plans after a couple of your opponent's moves. In terms of leadership, we're now living in chess times more than eagle times.

Leadership is more complex than ever, requiring leading beyond our means. As society becomes more mobile, dysfunctional, and competitive in vying for people's attention, leading has become more and more difficult. The rapid turnover of information, innovations, and competition means that to survive, a leader must look beyond himself or herself for answers. In secular arenas, better leadership means going beyond mere human wisdom and engaging one's soul, intuition, and discernment. For Christian leaders, it means looking beyond self to God. Just as multi-tasking has become necessary to keep pace in the twenty-first century, leaders must use multi-gifts and abilities as well. Challenging times require creative and insightful ideas. Nonlinear thinking includes input from spiritual resources. What better means to new ways of thinking and responding than getting in touch with the wisdom of God and his power?

Leadership requires greater people skills, a primary benefit of spiritual fruit. The leadership paradigm is actually changing as we move further into this century. In the old days, a leader could bark instructions to a naïve group of followers; based on his position alone, he could expect results. But the savvy attitudes of educated, less respectful, less committed, and more participatory followers today render industrial methods of leading impotent. More than ever, sophisticated people skills are vital to team building. The fruit of the Spirit provides a good starting list for dealing with relationships: "But the fruit of the Spirit is love, joy, peace, patience, kindness, good-ness, faithfulness, gentleness and self-control. Against such things there is no law. Since we live by the Spirit, let us keep in step with the Spirit" (Galatians 5:22-23,25). Many leaders lack strong people skills because they're primarily task ori-ented. For them, the added power of the fruit of the Spirit makes up for critical weak points. As a result, their followers feel loved and appreciated. Spiritual leaders use this resource as a way to motivate, recruit, and receive commitments from team members.

Postmodern people expect internal integrity rather than per-sonal segregation. In the past, leaders could separate their spir-itual/religious selves from what they did. They could avoid letting their personal beliefs interfere with their professional ones. In the twenty-first century, followers seek leaders who do not segment their life into compartments, but rather who are whole and authentic. Leaders who are spiritual can't sepa-rate their souls from leading. They're just as comfortable and natural in the office and at business meetings as they are in their worship and devotional lives. People who disengage their leading from their spirituality will be seen as hypocrites and as untrustworthy.

People recognize their own souls and seek the same of their leaders. In the past, you pretty much needed to leave your soul at the door when you came to work. This was even true of ministry at times. Business didn't acknowledge the spiritual side of people, and organizational life sometimes alienated people from their Creator. But as more and more people have become intrigued by the spiritual, they are seeking leaders and organizations that nurture their souls and the other parts of their lives. They won't be satisfied working for or being part of organizations that are in opposition to their spiritual health. People want more out of work and church. They want to find significance in what they do. They want to follow leaders who treat them as whole people who have hearts that need to be nourished and cared for. This means finding leaders who understand their needs and who are in tune with their own souls as they lead.

Leaders need internal strength to handle the pressures of modern leading. Situational ethics and competitive compromise cause many to go the route of organizational prostitution, selling their souls for the sake of success. One national news magazine asked the question on its cover, "Where have all the heroes gone?" People are looking for moral models who will be examples of integrity. Leaders are influencers, and when they say something, it has exponential impact. When they fail ethically and morally, it too has significant negative impact on the organization and on society as a whole. The pressures of conflict, competition, and change, plus the temptations of success, pride, and money, endanger even effective leaders.

Perhaps the greatest contemporary pressure is compressed time: having to multi-task while making more and more decisions in less and less time. Be fast or be left behind. This requires leaders to rely on autopilot, defaulting to character. Leading "in the zone" is a matter of leading from who you are. If a leader's character lacks moral and ethical fiber, his or her decisions will be weak and unreliable. Spiritual leaders are less apt to succumb to the pressures of leading because they are strong from the inside out. They're fixed to a different compass.

What Do We Mean by the Terms "Spiritual," "Leadership," and "Spiritual Leadership"?

One summer evening in a small Midwest town, two elderly women sat on a front porch, listening to the sounds of a church choir rehearsing down the block, intermingled with the chirping of the crickets. One woman said, "Isn't that a beautiful sound?"

The other responded, "Yes, and to think they do that by rubbing their legs together."

Defining terms can be pretty important. It helps us communicate clearly and avoid making wrong assumptions. Here are brief working definitions we will use as starting points, so that we share understanding through the rest of the book.

Leadership: By "leadership," we're referring to the social process in which people confer influence to individuals, so that those individuals can organize and assist the people in achieving what could not otherwise be accomplished. These individuals are known as leaders. Leadership is relational. Leaders don't "do" leadership. They lead, which hopefully catalyzes the leadership process.

Leadership is influence that people respond to voluntarily. Anything else is coercion, not leadership. Bullies don't lead; they intimidate. Leadership is influence, but not all influence is leadership—just as all dads are men, but not all men are dads.

Leadership is about people changing things as a group or team. It strategically aligns people with resources to accomplish mutual objectives. Management is about maintaining and doing things right. But leadership is about progressing and doing the right things. It involves power, resources, communication, vision, conflict, and people skills balanced with a task orientation.

Spiritual: By "spiritual," we mean that every person was created with a soul—a spiritual dimension that exists in addition to the body and mind. This is what the Bible refers to as being made in the image of God. The soul transcends personality and temperament, although it is affected by and influences them. Because I have chosen Christian boundaries for this book, I would say that God is external to humans in their natural condition, that only through faith can we receive and live by God's Spirit. This approach is counter to popular trends today, which say we are all gods or that god is internal. This popular view lends itself to our self-centered tendencies and reflects the biblical idea that the initial sin was striving to become like the gods. It's akin to putting the fox in charge of the chicken coop.

Be leery when people create belief systems that cater to their own motivations. Our souls are our direct link to God and the supernatural, much like a power cord is a way to tap the AC electricity in your home or office. Our souls are designed to affect all other aspects of ourselves, such as our body and mind, but they are unique in function and development. In other words, you can grow physically, intellectually, and even emotionally, and still be a spiritual neophyte. Yet, as we grow spiritually, we will see how our actions, thoughts, attitudes, and relationships develop as a result.

Spiritual leadership: This is the intersection of the above characteristics, where individuals are spiritually in tune with God and living under his direction, as well as gifted and skilled as persons of influence among others. Although the rest of this book seeks to explain and better define spiritual leadership, we'll build on this brief definition.

Spiritual leadership isn't just about being more spiritual than others. Everyone can become a spiritual person and grow in that aspect of his or her life. God has given us leaders, specifically as a way to catalyze growth and change in churches, businesses, and organizations so that others can be more fulfilled and served. Spiritual leadership isn't just about leaders who have a personal faith or who claim to be spiritual. It is about bringing together the two elements so that spirituality maximizes leading in ways that nothing else can.

While leading can ruin our souls if we let it, it isn't unholy. In fact, it's a noble call—a vocation that God desires to bless and empower with spiritual resources. Leadership is God's way of caring for the needs of the whole. When we lead poorly, many suffer. Non-spiritual leadership is inadequate for today's environment. Relying on God and the spiritual resources he provides can preserve you during the kinds of difficult situations leaders find themselves in. The risks of leadership are high, but the benefits are significant.

The needs of the twenty-first century call for us to lead with power and wisdom beyond our own resources. Now, more than ever, we need courageous men and women who understand what it means to lead from their minds and souls.

A Definition of Leadership

What is a leader?

How is leadership different from management?

How is twenty-first-century leadership different from its predecessor?

How can you tell if someone is a leader?

How can you measure someone's leading ability?

What are the qualities and benefits of authentic leadership?

What are some of the unspoken expectations people have of leaders?

What Is a Leader?

So you want to be a better leader. When people use the term "leadership," what do they mean? Some gurus in the field of leadership want you to think that everything rises and falls on leadership. But rest assured; everything in life is not about leadership, just as everyone is not wired to lead. Leadership is a social relationship in which people allow individuals to influence them toward intentional change. Leadership involves more than leaders and what they do. Power ultimately resides in the followers or collaborators.

Leaders are indivudals who are able to see and articulate vision, pursue change through aligning people with resources, and organize people and systems to accomplish these objectives. Leadership is influence, but not all influence is leadership.

Because we're analyzing the intersection of spirituality and leadership, it may help us to briefly look at the characteristics of each of the intersecting avenues. In the Introduction, we gave you the penny explanation of leadership. Now let's take time for a dime definition. (We'll define spirituality more deeply in section 2.)

Definition: Leadership is the social process in which people confer influence to individuals, so that they can organize and assist the people in achieving what could not otherwise be accomplished.

Leadership deals with relationships—people working with each other toward a common objective. The word "process" means that leadership is not so much what is achieved, but *how* things are achieved. There are multiple ways to achieve goals, such as through individual accomplishments, managerial processes, or coercive means.

Again, the true power-holders in leadership are actually the followers and collaborators, not the leaders. When people in charge don't receive power voluntarily, then it's not leadership. When people don't allow leaders to have influence, the leader isn't a leader at all. Such a leader is merely a figurehead—a person who thinks he or she is leading when the one following is just out for a walk.

A leader is the individual with the most influence in a group; the influence is given by group members so that the entire group can achieve more together. Someone must cast vision, organize, and catalyze the group to achieve. True democratic processes, where everyone has equal influence, are chaotic and inefficient, if at all effective. For example, the United States is called a democracy, but functions primarily as a republic, where elected representatives lead and manage. Leaders are given the authority to catalyze followers to pursue common goals. Leaders are catalysts—change agents who stir the pot and facilitate the use of group member talents and resources.

While this explanation may imply that groups get together with common goals and then find leaders to help them achieve them, the sequence isn't actually important. Sometimes an individual with an idea or vision can cast it to people to see if he or she can gather people around that goal. What happens first is not as important as the fact that leadership involves people working together toward accomplishments that individually they couldn't achieve.

By the term "common goals," I don't mean that everyone necessarily has the same personal goals, but that through group accomplishments, people can fulfill their individual aspirations at the same time as the group's goals are met. The goal of leading is ultimately synergy, where the cumulative effect of the members working together is greater than the sum of the members working individually.

A quick aside: Because leadership is not what leaders *do*, we should address a common myth regarding leadership mentoring. Some people believe that one of the best ways to create new leaders is for them to shadow a leader and observe leadership. The problem with this logic is that at any given time, a person who leads may not be leading. Mentoring is vital, but should include open discussions regarding which situations require leadership and which do not. Like most of us, leaders wear multiple hats. Sometimes a person who leads is teaching, or managing, or being a father/husband or wife/mother. At other times, a person who leads is being a friend, or a child of God, or a follower on another team. To understand leadership, you need to be able to discern when a leader is actually leading. That, in and of itself, is part of the trick.

Leaders are people who consistently recognize when leading is needed. Effective leaders act in situationally appropriate ways. When leading is required, selling, managing, or any other role is ineffective. Or leading may be intermixed with other activities. For example, leaders may be leading as they teach, if it has to do with establishing organizational priorities, values, or vision. That is why learning how to lead is such a complex challenge.

The story is told of two bricklayers working on a building. When someone asked the first laborer what he was making, the man responded, "Fifteen dollars an hour." When the other man was asked what he was making, he answered, "A cathedral that will point people to God." That man was fired, because he was supposed to be building a garage.

The twist of the joke reminds us that a key to success in leading others is appropriateness. Leading is far more artistic than mechanical. The following list of questions shows how leaders discern where leading is required.

- *Is significant change needed?* Leaders are authors of change when and where it's needed. When the change is not just designed for maintenance and is more than incremental, then leading is required.

- *Does the change affect the entire organization?* If so, leading is necessary. Piecemeal improvements are not unimportant, but probably require management and administration more than leading. When a person, plan, or circumstance will influence the culture and nature of the larger group, then a leader needs to be involved.

- *Does this involve vision and core values?* These are the basic building blocks of leading.

- *Will this affect the organization long term?* Temporary influence may be a factor in some leadership situations, but any sort of enduring impact definitely should be a leader's concern.

- *Does this have to do with team member morale?* The primary asset of any leader is his or her ability to align people with tasks. When motivation, esprit de corps, or teamwork issues arise, a leader should act.

- *Does this have to do with macro systems or the structure of the organization?* Micro issues need not engage leading, but big-picture issues are calls for a leader's involvement.

- *Will this change the culture of the organization?* Culture is the environment people work in. It affects their attitude, enjoyment, productivity, and overall approach to accomplishing their tasks. Leaders are shepherds of organizational culture.

HOW IS LEADERSHIP DIFFERENT FROM MANAGEMENT?

For a time, a lot of leadership literature bashed management, labeling it "ineffective leadership." So people preferred to use the term "leading" when they were talking about managing, because the latter wasn't in vogue.

The problem is in using the terms interchangeably. A bad apple is not a banana. There are good and bad apples and there are good and bad bananas. They're just different fruits. In the same way, leadership is different from management. Bad leadership isn't management; it's just bad leadership. Good management isn't leadership; it's just good management.

Both terms have to do with supervision and decision making within organizations. Management is primarily about maintenance, establishing balance, and keeping an organization functioning day to day. Leadership is about making changes, pursuing new ventures, and cultivating a strong vision within the culture. Organizations always need good management. They only need leadership when change is required. By trying to change things that aren't broken, leaders can actually do damage to organizations that are functioning well. But with the multitude of changes happening in the twenty-first century, leaders are in demand more than ever.

Usually, leadership and management are kissing cousins, but not identical twins. At times, they feud, because management and leadership can be counterproductive to each other. Management seeks to maintain and to reject influences that would change an organization; leadership strives to change and reject status quo, especially when maintenance spells long-term dysfunction or death. Systems such as government bureaucracies are strong because they're designed to preserve themselves and thus retard the ability of a despot or rogue group of anarchists who would significantly influence them negatively. The problem, as you can imagine, is that they also work against positive people seeking constructive change.

This is all akin to the natural immune systems in a body. The very antibodies that reject germs and preserve health can also reject organ transplants that save people. Managerial mazes are often antithetical to leadership, and this can frustrate leaders who want to bring about changes designed to benefit people.

Recruiting and training leaders is a process different from developing managers. Often, leaders don't fit well in traditional classroom structures and tend to avoid pure left-brain thinking. Although leaders sometimes oversee managers, very few are actually wired to manage. Effective leaders understand that they need to know their weaknesses, and they then gather people and resources around them so their organization can run effectively. Leadership and management require distinctly different dispositions; it's extremely rare to find individuals gifted in both arenas. Managers tend to obtain their identity heavily from the organization they serve. While this book values the importance of good-quality management, our focus is specifically about leadership, leaders, and leading with excellence, ideally from a spiritual orientation.

When I was a boy, my dad taught me an important life lesson one day as we stood in a soybean field. "What's that?" he asked, pointing to a tall green plant.

I looked at him sheepishly and responded, "You know what that is. It's a cornstalk."

"No, it's a weed," he said.

"Dad, that's not a weed. We have acres of corn. That is corn."

Dad answered, "But a cornstalk in a soybean field is a weed."

When managing is required, leading is a weed. When leading is needed, managing is a weed. The key is appropriateness, understanding what's needed and doing what it takes to respond effectively. Those with a higher degree of leading aptitude know when and where leading is required and are able to lead at that time. To lead when you should be teaching, managing, marketing, and following is dysfunctional. To manage, market, teach, and follow when you should be leading also reflects incompetence.

How Is Twenty-First-Century Leadership Different from Its Predecessor?

While the objective of twenty-first-century leadership is the same as twentieth-century leadership—to accomplish goals through groups rather than individuals—the process has changed. Twentieth-century leadership tended to center around industry-oriented, autocratic, white males. While top-down, unidirectional leading may fit bygone eras or small segments of contemporary society where crises and antiquated cultural conditions reward this style, post-industrial leadership is different and more demanding. How?

Education: With the increase in levels of education, people desire to participate. They're much less likely to take commands from a single source. Educated people want to be considered as collaborators. The role of leaders is to harness the brain trust and merge the cumulative experience, wisdom, and insight of the participants.

Information: In the age of multi-lane information superhighways, leaders simply can't know everything they need to lead, and they must rely on others. Leaders used to be able to control information to their benefit. Now no one has a corner on information. Multiple sources of information and team insights require leaders to gather input from multiple people, calling for more relational skills.

Women: The rise of education among women and the fact that they have been mainstreamed into the workforce has resulted in a kinder, gentler form of leading. Women tend to be more process-oriented while their male counterparts tend to be more outcome-driven. Women often are more inclusive of people and more relational as a whole. This requires leadership to include more dialogue and group discussion, less monologue or lecture.

Democratization: In our culture—and in many around the world—people say, "I want my vote to count." Dictatorial leaders are not valued or are disdained, even if they're loving. Most people want to participate in decisions that impact the group.

Organizational complexity: Many organizations are big and complex. Even small companies and organizations face more competition than ever. These make leading a more difficult task than it was in static, simpler times. A single individual rarely has the knowledge to face the challenges.

Fragmented loyalties: Twenty-first-century people are inundated with opportunities, stress, and challenges. They're mobile, as well as disconnected from the extended family and traditional villages where people once lived large chunks of their lives. This "every man for himself" mentality requires leaders to be more servant-like and to emphasize relationships and offer connection with others as a meaningful benefit. With so many voices competing for allegiance, leaders have less influence and therefore must behave more congenially, yet assertively and creatively.

How Can You Tell If Someone Is a Leader?

Americans especially don't like to think there are things they cannot do. Because it's "a free country," they believe anything is obtainable. Motivational speakers and writers tell us that if we try hard enough, we can reach our goal, no matter how far-fetched it may be.

Of course, we know better. If you're a forty-five-year-old, five-foot-ten, two-hundred-pound couch potato who dreams of playing in the NBA, guess what? It ain't gonna happen!

When society elevates the value of leading and authors give the impression that anyone can be a leader, a lot of people are set up to be frustrated. Some teachers go so far as to suggest that everyone is a leader, even if we lead only ourselves. But if we go back to our definition of leadership as a social process of catalyzing groups to act together, the only way you could lead yourself is if you have multiple personalities. If that's the case, you need therapy, not leadership training.

Effective leaders demonstrate initiative, vision, and self-discipline, all of which are important individual traits to possess. But having these characteristics does not make someone a leader. If everyone were a leader, there'd be chaos. Only a small percentage of people are wired to lead and a few others can develop leader skills, but the majority of people will never be leaders, regardless of what motivators want us to believe.

Okay, so how do you discern if someone has the capacity to be a leader?

Look at early history. While some leaders discover their gifts as adults, many leadership gifts can be seen on school playgrounds, in classrooms, and on Little League fields. Watching a person as a child or delving into his or her childhood or adolescent background can reveal gifts of influence. Captain of the basketball team, student body president, class monitor, or church youth group leader are examples of early indicators of leader wiring.

Who do people listen to? Watch a group of people and notice that an inordinate amount of attention goes to one or two individuals. But don't confuse leaders with those who simply like the sound of their own voice. Instead, look for people others watch and pay close attention to. When a meeting is taking place and a leader is silent, someone is apt to say, "Joan, what do you think about this?" "John, give us your opinion."

Who is missed? When leaders are absent, there is often a sense of loss, the awareness of an empty chair. While other people may be loved and appreciated, they are often rarely noticed when absent. "Where's Joe today?" "I haven't seen Debbie this week." Regular comments such as these often reflect leader influence.

Look at group goal accomplishment. Is the person currently being followed by others? Some individuals consistently emerge as overseers of others. Do people answer to them at work? Are they able to recruit and sustain groups? Can they take an event and run with it?

Consider troublemakers. Sometimes we overlook people who may appear critical or opinionated because they irritate us. Ironically, a sign of leadership is having an opinion and wanting to do something about it. Frustrated, underutilized leaders are sometimes overlooked because other leaders see them as antagonistic.

How Can You Measure Someone's Leading Ability?

Moses didn't see himself as a natural leader, so he asked God to provide a spokesperson (Aaron) when God wouldn't let him off the hook. The priest who anointed young David as king didn't see his capacity for leading at the start. The Bible and history give us many examples of insecure leaders who exterminated people who they saw as threats. These were likely well-networked, ambitious people who found themselves in positions of leadership, but without the capacity to fulfill the responsibilities.

Some people have a great capacity to lead, but perhaps have never developed it. Others have less capacity, but are maximizing their potential in that area and therefore may be perceived as strong leaders. The ability to accurately estimate capacity is more rare than leading itself. Many good-quality leaders are overlooked because of their youth or because we've never seen them in a leadership situation.

An equal but opposite challenge is to help a person understand when he or she is not leader material. Because of the misperception that there is an aura of joy around leading, many are self-deceived wannabes who don't feel self-worth unless considered a leader. "You've never given me a chance," is an oft-heard complaint among those who think that leadership is some sort of formal role or position. But leaders with natural gifts intuitively seek conditions where they can express their leading, or they find themselves in roles where people thrust leading responsibilities upon them.

Once while I was playing follow-the-leader with my five-year-old, he said, "Dad, wait for me. I'm the leader." Interestingly, that attitude is common among adults who want to lead, but who lack the skills and/or capacity to lead to a significant degree. In some ways, leaders cannot *not* lead. As they participate in groups, people quickly perceive their leading abilities. That's why leaders who don't want to get involved sometimes stay along the fringes. While others see them as aloof or uncommitted, these people have discovered that when they participate as followers, peers recognize their leader gifts and often thrust them into responsibilities they don't desire. Other times, the existing leader perceives these natural leaders as a threat, such as when people begin seeking the advice of the participant instead of talking to the "real" leader.

One of the best measures of leader aptitude may surprise you. Many people look at the sheer size of the organization that a leader oversees, assuming this is a good measure of capacity. While this can be a factor to consider, some people with mediocre leadership gifts can manipulate their way into key positions. Political prowess, an established network, seniority, and sometimes even luck help people find key roles where leading is expected but may not reflect their gifting. Never assume that the person holding the CEO office space is wired to lead. The better question is, "How did this person come to this place?"

A more effective gauge of leadership ability is to analyze who makes up the followers. The caliber of people on a team is often a better reflection of leadership ability than the number of people on a team. When sharp, talented, and even strong leaders make up the constituency, chances are you have a leader of leaders at the helm. Quality people and other leaders rarely have the patience to follow someone lacking leadership qualities.

WHAT ARE THE QUALITIES AND BENEFITS OF AUTHENTIC LEADERSHIP?

Okay, let's head down the grocery store soup aisle. See the cans of chili? Look at the labels. Some of them say *con carne,* meaning "with meat." These cans have beef or chicken in addition to beans and sauce.

Carne is the root of the word "incarnation," which refers to the physical manifestation of God in the flesh, Jesus. Leadership *con carne* has to do with the merger of being and doing. Incarnational leading is where leader and leading become one, where we lead primarily out of who we are as opposed to what we know, what we can do, and what position we hold. This version of leading has definite benefits; and it requires a leader to focus on his or her character, soul, and inner life.

WYSIWYG is a computer acronym for "What you see is what you get," referring to the exact likeness between what is on the screen and what you get on a hard copy. Early computer programs could drive us simple people nuts, because we had to guess what the end product would look like when we were trying to create a document or graphic.

In a similar way, leaders create tension among followers when they're not what they appear to be. Authenticity means the real deal, not a façade or mock character. Pretending to be someone we're not is quite common among the general public, but it becomes disastrous in leaders because of the impact they have upon society. If we sell ourselves to be something other than what we are, we're being manipulative and misleading. Leaders who say one thing and do another, who seem one way but perform differently, lower trust and disintegrate the cohesiveness of a team or organization.

As leaders, we're in the business of selling ourselves, intentionally and unintentionally. People buy into our talents, vision, and competence. If they don't, we cease to be leaders. When we portray ourselves as something we're not, we are seen as inauthentic. Sometimes we don't learn this until it's too late. Chinks in our armor eventually emerge over time and under pressure. When people place their trust in leaders with deep faults, they are likely to face disappointment and defeat.

Leaders benefit from authentic leading. Authenticity reduces stress. Maintaining an air of being someone we are not can be very stressful. Duplicity takes a lot of energy to maintain. Just as certain software programs take up a lot of memory on a computer and cause the machine to bog down, pretenses soak up huge amounts of space in our psyche. They require us to worry about what people are thinking and who might see us; we can't just be ourselves. Instead of one life, we're living two or more. We find it difficult to relax because we're forever "on." We fear that if people see us when we're not "on," they'll discover who we really are and lose respect for us. Decision making becomes more difficult because we wrestle with a variety of values and perceptions. Under pressure, people resort to their basic fabric. Authentic leaders find it easier to make the tough calls that arise because they are who they appear to be.

When I was a boy, wood was more prevalent than today. In wood shop class, we could order all sorts of solid stock to make our projects. Today, solid stock furniture is harder to find and very expensive. Most wood used today is a type of laminate, which manufacturers make by tightly gluing together particles or very thin layers of wood to form a single board. The problem with cheaper laminates is that they tend to come apart over time. Similarly, laminated leaders peel apart during times of pressure and when social forces pull them in conflicting directions. When leader being and leader doing become separate processes, we reduce our ability for peak performance.

Whenever we talk about authenticity, we also need to discuss integrity. Both are quality issues. Authenticity has to do with being genuine rather than artificial. Integrity pertains to the quality of unity and completeness. It means "whole," "one," "complete." The word "integer" comes from the same root and refers to a whole number as opposed to a fraction, which is incomplete.

If a bad person does evil deeds, this person is a person of integrity in the literal sense. The insides match the outsides. The opposite is true as well. The benefit of integrity is that behavior is predictable—you get what you see. Predicting values, actions, and decisions is important for anyone, but it is especially vital for leaders because their influence is far greater than that of most people.

WHAT ARE SOME OF THE UNSPOKEN EXPECTATIONS PEOPLE HAVE OF LEADERS?

Ever wonder why leading is such a difficult job? It's messy because there are so many intangibles tied to it, many of which go unspoken. Most leadership books and seminars begin from the standpoint of the leader. But if the leader's role is to serve people by organizing and catalyzing them as a group, it would be helpful to look at leadership from the perspective of the followers and collaborators. While most leadership books deal with the practices of organizations, they tend to be weak on the soft side of leading, on the people skills it takes to lead. Spiritual leadership emphasizes the soft side of leading, because spirituality has a lot to do with relationships. Though we'll look at leadership skills more deeply in section 7, it might help to have a basic understanding of leaders and relationships here.

Besides the organizational components of leading (i.e., vision casting, team building, conflict management), leaders regularly face emotional factors with the people they lead. For example, many followers seek emotional fulfillment from their leaders. Leaders provide this with one of their "hats." A "hat" is usually defined as a social role. We commonly refer to busy people as "wearing many hats," meaning they fill a variety of roles within an organization or community. For isntance, you might be a father, friend, pastor, writer, coach, boss, husband, son, and follower. In each role, you put on a different hat. When roles overlap, you'll often experience tension internally and in how people respond to you. The many names for God in the Old Testament portray the array of hats he wears. These correspond to his characteristics and responses in specific situations.

Leaders wear a variety of hats as well. Followers and collaborators can expect certain behaviors and attitudes that will either add to or detract from a leader's effectiveness, depending on how he or she responds. The challenge is that nearly all of these hats are intangible. Certainly, they're rarely discussed. They tend to be felt or intuitive instead. Leaders who are perceptive are able to don the right hat and respond appropriately. When leaders are aloof to these expectations or are slow to respond, they lose credibility and influence, and their leadership is weakened as a result. A leader may need to change hats from meeting to meeting, or even respond differently in a single setting to people with various expectations and needs. The ability to wear a variety of hats increases a leader's effectiveness.

While the list of hats varies from person to person and situation to situation, here's a short list of the more common hats that leaders are expected to wear at specific times. Understanding these helps explain why a leader gains or loses the loyalty of people.

Parent—security and direction. Remember that wonderful feeling or presence you felt as a child when Mom and Dad were home? And remember that inverse sensation when your parents were absent? Something was missing. This parental presence is more prevalent than most of us realize and would probably admit, because we think we don't need parents anymore. Leaders often fulfill emotional desires within organizations that are similar to how parents nurture families. This has little to do with age or even the maturity of members. Effective organizations have a family component to them; families long for a parent to provide direction, security, and a sense of togetherness. Maintaining a loving bond between siblings (or other team members) and working out differences is a parental role as well. When leaders fail to understand this or dismiss it because "we're all adults here," they leave unmet needs in the people they serve; and as a result they weaken leadership.

Police—safety and stability. Every organization or team at times needs to know that an authority figure will keep the peace and provide a safe environment. If bullies arise or people are at odds with each other, a leader needs to don a police hat and "break it up." Policing a team will be minimal among more mature people, but sometimes the best of us can use some outside governance. Keeping the rules, obeying standard operating procedures, and establishing a peaceful community isn't easy, but it's often needed for leadership to thrive. Leaders who are uncomfortable with this hat can alienate people and lose control. But at critical times, policing a group can raise commitment.

Judge—justice and authority. While sometimes a leader fulfills a police officer role by keeping peace and promoting a safe environment, at other times a leader must don the robe of a judge. This happens when organizational policy is tested, when there is a difference of opinion between two collaborators, or when wisdom and polity clarification are needed. Running from tough calls or delegating leader decisions reflects a lack of courage. A leader who can't make a decision or who is unwilling to make tough calls will lose respect and diminish leadership. Many leadership moments aren't black and white—they're subjective; and while you might make a wrong decision, indecision is usually an even worse choice.

Counselor—ear and wisdom. Effective leaders must become counselors at times, because working with people means more than just employing their talents. People bring emotional baggage, traumas, life conflicts, and the challenge of personal decision making with them to the organization. If you'll deal only with items directly related to the organization or task at hand, you'll be ineffective as a leader and disappointing to those you lead. Taking time out to listen, provide counsel, and interrupt the flow of a task process can stress out those who are wired to accomplish. But a farmer doesn't keep plowing when the machinery is broken. He or she must at least stop to assess the damage to see whether or not to continue. Leaders who refuse to get involved in the personal lives of those they lead reduce the respect and loyalty of their followers.

Friend—enjoyment and encouragement. Effective leaders are rarely best friends with those they lead, but they must wear the friend hat at strategic times. This goes beyond token congeniality or mere social etiquette. Sometimes you don't need a parent, counselor, or police officer; you need a friend. A leader needs humility if he or she is to be more of a peer and less of a boss. Writing a personal thank-you note, sending a birthday card, helping a team member move, playing sports together, or just hanging out in a coffee shop are all friend situations that endear people to you as a leader. If you don't know how to behave as a friend when it's appropriate, you'll diminish your ability to enjoy people and to encourage them personally.

One caution here is that people will often misread your friendliness as a desire for you to be close friends. Most of us have a natural desire to be close to leaders, whether it's to be in the inner circle, to associate with someone of influence, or merely because people often build one-way emotional ties with those who lead. True friendship must be mutual. Close friends rarely allow us to wear hats that deviate from the friend hat. This means that leaders must be able to move from hat to hat within a leadership situation.

Coach—motivation and training. Coaching and leading have a lot in common, but a leader is not always a coach. When problems arise and team members need assistance in determining a course of action, the coach hat becomes necessary. When players lack sufficient knowledge or skills, training must happen. But coaches are not just strategic technicians. They're also part cheerleader. Shaking the pom-poms and shouting "atta boy," "nice job," "we can do it," are all vital roles that periodically emerge in leadership. The leader who fails to give advice or provide encouragement is slacking.

Understanding when to put on this hat is important. A person who only cheers loses credibility. A leader who is always coaching rarely raises up a team that can think and function on its own.

Pastor—moral guidance and inspiration. Spiritual leaders have a significant advantage when it comes to this leader hat. Looking out for the spiritual well-being and inner person is a key function of leaders. Spiritual leaders in the secular marketplace might feel uncomfortable with the role of shepherding, but people often need moral guidance and spiritual inspiration, which only comes from divine means. Leaders work with whole people, not just bodies and brains. They can't sever the souls from those they lead. Certain situations call for leaders to behave like priests, pastors, and spiritual guides. It can be crucial to pray for and with a coworker, or to employ scriptural insights or rely on godly wisdom. Leaders are in the people-building business. Helping people grow can require moral and spiritual input. Failure to recognize these situations or avoiding them due to incompetence or reticence will diminish leadership strength.

Leaders can't be all things to all people, but they must strive to wear the different hats their leadership position requires. Knowing your limitations is one thing, but hiding from the various hats that situations demand is another. Rarely will people verbalize their need for you to wear one of these hats. They're probably not in touch with these intangible emotions, but they long for you to address them as their leader. If you don't meet their expectations in these areas, it will diminish your perceived competence and weaken your collaborators' loyalty to you.

When a leader loses influence, it's easy to point to tangible reasons for the demise. But underlying many of these symptoms are deeper issues of group members' unmet emotional needs and feelings of abandonment or violation. As we'll discuss more in section 3, the spiritual leader must rely heavily on discernment and sensitivity to the Spirit's leading, and on a godly willingness and ability to respond appropriately, because people matter so much to God.

A Definition of Spirituality

What are the various levels of spirituality?

What causes us to possess but not employ the Spirit?

What's the dominant characteristic of a spiritual person?

What's the difference between spiritual leaders and religious zealots?

WHAT ARE THE VARIOUS LEVELS OF SPIRITUALITY?

What does it mean to be a spiritual person in the broadest sense? Throughout history, most societies have recognized that they possess a dimension that transcends the physical realm and is more than mere mental and emotional functions. The spiritual realm has its own energy, activity, value, and practices.

One way to look at spirituality is to break it down into four basic levels of acknowledgment. Most anyone who claims to be spiritual is somewhere along this continuum in terms of recognizing spirituality.

Level 1: There is a spiritual realm that transcends the physical. This most basic level of spirituality acknowledges that a spiritual, nonphysical, or spatial dimension exists that is every bit as real as the physical realm. But this spiritual dimension can't be measured or quantified by the same instruments. This realm transcends the five senses.

Level 2: Every human has a spiritual dimension centered in the soul. This level of spirituality identifies a soul within each person. An inner sense of destiny as demonstrated by the will to survive a concentration camp or even mindless work activities reveals the existence of something more than the mirror reflects. Just as a valve stem is the apparatus to get air into a tire, our soul is the vehicle to connect with the spiritual realm.

Level 3: A deity exists who connects with us spiritually. This level recognizes the existence of a deity, a being who transcends the limitations of our souls, but who provides a connection with us through the port of our souls. Personal or impersonal, this god(s) helps us better understand truth and the root of our spirituality.

Level 4: We define who the deity is and how the deity wants to connect with us. At this level, we see huge divisions among people. Those who dislike tension between differing belief systems simply suggest that everyone is right. The problem with believing that every truth is sufficient so long as it is earnestly followed, or that all belief systems lead to the same place, is that once you get beyond a superficial level, many of these ideologies contradict each other. Christianity, for example, precludes the idea that you can be a follower of Christ and others. Jesus said, "I am the way and the truth and the life. No one comes to the Father except through me" (John 14:6). He blatantly included all who believe in him and overtly excluded all other belief systems.

A popular practice is to cherry-pick favorite ideas from a multitude of spiritual belief systems, concocting one's own homegrown recipe. Human nature has the tendency to skew truth according to its selfish ways. We avoid things that stifle us and we embrace ideals that feed our desires and passions.

Unfortunately, when we cut and paste our spiritual beliefs, we ruin them. Removing an oxygen atom from harmless carbon dioxide gas gives you an entirely different substance—poisonous carbon monoxide. Scrapbook religion is self-deceptive in that we think we know enough to create our own truth, believing the elements we've borrowed from other belief systems are reliable. The fastest way to ruin a spiritual belief system is to sift it with your personal screens, leaving out what you don't like and combining a concoction of self-edited ideas.

How do you know which spiritual belief system is right? If this is such an important part of life, how can you be certain you're making the right choice? You can't. No matter how much you dissect, study, research, explain, and reason, the bottom line is that any spiritual belief system requires faith. Trying to avoid all risks is actually antithetical to spirituality, because faith is a part of our soul's function and is needed for well-being.

Let's say you place two chairs within eighteen inches of each other and you stand, straddling each chair. One foot is on a chair representing known truth and the other on the chair symbolizing what you don't know about God. The gap between the two represents faith.

Many people say that they don't buy the concept of faith; they want proof. But faith is a part of authentic spirituality. Even most non-spiritual, everyday activities require faith from us. We have faith that the restaurant that serves us will not poison us. We have faith that the person coming at us in the opposing lane will not cross the thin yellow line. We have faith that we will live another month, so we go to work to pay the bills and don't get stressed out about saying good-bye to friends and loved ones. We can't really be sure of any of these things, yet we accept them on faith. We're constantly making assumptions, bridging the gap of what we hope for and what we know with practical faith.

Now faith is being sure of what we hope for and certain of what we do not see. (Hebrews 11:1)

As stated in the Introduction, I've chosen to employ the values of orthodox Christianity as portrayed in the Bible to define the idea of spirituality in this book. The Bible states that we all have the God-given option of free will. We can determine what we believe and, for the most part, how we choose to live our lives. Whether you decide to follow the teachings of the Koran, the Book of Mormon, Buddha, Confucius, or some other personal favorite, that is your right. But because the idea of spirituality is difficult enough to define within any of these belief systems, not yielding to a single one is impractical and unrealistic if you want to learn what it means to be spiritual, let alone a spiritual leader.

If you try to play baseball with the rules of basketball or football, everyone's going to be frustrated. Deciding what kind of game you're playing is important if you want to be effective in terms of spiritual leadership. People who mix and match their spirituality are like people trying to play baseball with a basketball on a football field. Besides confusing team members and fans, you're not going to be very productive.

While we all have souls and we are spiritual regardless of our relationship with God, we lack fervency apart from him. His spiritual life force is what makes us alive. Marathon runners understand the concept of "second wind." When they feel as though they've hit the wall and can go no farther, their body begins to rejuvenate itself, providing a sense of freshness without ever stopping. When God created humanity, he breathed life into Adam (Genesis 2:7). When he breathes on our dusty souls, we gain a second wind. The spiritual person, in God's eyes, is someone who has his or her second spiritual wind.

WHAT CAUSES US TO POSSESS BUT NOT EMPLOY THE SPIRIT?

Often people welcome God into their lives, only to leave him boxed up in the garage next to the Christmas decorations.

Americans, especially, are collectors. They gather baseball cards, cars, antiques, books, and countless other possessions. One interesting thing about collecting is that although you possess items, you do not use them. They receive no wear and tear. We even encourage others not to disturb our collections: "Just look; don't touch." It appears that we often take that attitude with our spiritual lives as well. We're "collectors" of God's Spirit. We dust off our idea of him once a week or so, talk about him among fellow collectors, and at times long for him to become a routine part of our lives.

For the most part, we lock God's Spirit away from our everyday world. Unfortunately, without use our spiritual power dwindles like a car engine that needs to be started every so often, or a bicycle tire that goes flat for lack of riding, or a house that becomes a shambles without attention. The solution is that we need to make God's Spirit a part of our everyday functions, just as we eat, sleep, work, and communicate. We need to intersect our work, home, community, and sexuality with God as well. We must intermix the realms. Whatever God touches becomes sacred. Spirituality that isn't 24/7 is just hollow religion—a segregated component of a nonintegrated person. Spiritual people are usually religious, but religious people are often not spiritual.

Many people keep their spirituality on blocks in the garage, or framed in a shadow box hanging on the wall, crated up neatly in the attic of their souls. Like unused exercise equipment purchased around the New Year, we think of the Spirit as a wonderful thing, but we push him off to a corner of our lives as we maintain life on our own. Instead of paying the price to exercise, we avoid the hassle of learning a new "system" of behaving. And in addition to our lack of discipline and our procrastination, we face the spiritual dimension of opposing forces.

So I say, live by the Spirit, and you will not gratify the
desires of the sinful nature. For the sinful nature desires

what is contrary to the Spirit, and the Spirit what is contrary to the sinful nature. They are in conflict with each other, so that you do not do what you want. (Galatians 5:16-17)

WHAT'S THE DOMINANT CHARACTERISTIC OF A SPIRITUAL PERSON?

Those who belong to Christ Jesus have crucified the sinful nature with its passions and desires. Since we live by the Spirit, let us keep in step with the Spirit. (Galatians 5:24-25)

A spiritual person is someone who continues to let go of the self-focus that is antithetical to God. Spiritual people must kiss their self-oriented premonitions farewell. In addition to sacrificing our self-willed lives, we must keep cadence with the Spirit. The beat we walked to yesterday may be different today. Being creatures of habit, we tend to replicate what we did in times before instead of flowing with God's Spirit.

But at times God changes speed, perhaps to see if we are paying attention to him. I remember our band teacher in high school constantly telling us to "watch me, watch me," so that we would keep our tempo in unison, fast or slow. Because what God desires most from us is a relationship, it shouldn't surprise us that he tells us to watch him.

Then Jesus was led by the Spirit into the desert to be tempted by the devil. (Matthew 4:1)

"And now, compelled by the Spirit, I [Paul] am going to Jerusalem, not knowing what will happen to me there." (Acts 20:22)

If leaders like Jesus and Paul saw the need to follow the leading of the Spirit, who are we to do anything less? Sometimes these leadings transcend human logic: "to be tempted by the devil"; to go "not knowing what will happen." At times, spiritual people end up doing things that are illogical or even outlandish. The Bible is full of these examples. To be weird, overly risky, or blatantly stupid certainly isn't the equivalent to spiritual living. History is full of people who blamed their irresponsible actions on God's leading. God doesn't contradict himself. He won't lead us against his stated guidelines or character.

The big difference between people who are spiritually authentic and those who are wannabes is that the former follow when the Spirit leads them into deserts and potentially dangerous scenarios. The fainthearted pull back, justify avoiding deserts, and plot their own trails. But once we start pulling back on the reins, we find it easier to do it each successive time. Spiritual people fight this temptation and submit to God's leadings.

"God is spirit, and his worshipers must worship in spirit and in truth." (John 4:24)

Spiritual people recognize that we are spiritual peas in physical pods. We're not designed to think or live purely in the physical dimension. God created us in his image, meaning that we are spiritual in nature. While we're tempted to turn what is tangible into gods, we must fight the urge. Spiritual people develop skill sets that allow them to connect in the non-physical dimension where they worship God and center on truth. Spiritual people pay the price of constantly honing their spiritual aptitudes. They switch to a new paradigm, with new frameworks for thinking, prioritizing, and fitting the pieces of life together.

Those who live according to the sinful nature have their minds set on what that nature desires; but those who live in accordance with the Spirit have their minds set on what the Spirit desires. The mind of sinful man is death, but the mind controlled by the Spirit is life and peace; the sinful mind is hostile to God. It does not sub-mit to God's law, nor can it do so. Those controlled by the sinful nature cannot please God.

You, however, are controlled not by the sinful nature but by the Spirit, if the Spirit of God lives in you. And if anyone does not have the Spirit of Christ, he does not belong to Christ. But if Christ is in you, your body is dead because of sin, yet your spirit is alive because of righteousness. And if the Spirit of him who raised Jesus from the dead is living in you, he who raised Christ from the dead will also give life to your mortal bodies through his Spirit, who lives in you. . . .

For if you live according to the sinful nature, you will die; but if by the Spirit you put to death the misdeeds of the body, you will live, because those who are led by the Spirit of God are sons of God. For you did not receive a spirit that makes you a slave again to fear, but you received the Spirit of sonship. And by him we cry, "Abba, Father." The Spirit himself testifies with our spirit that we are God's children. (Romans 8:5-11,13-16)

This passage is the Christian version of the Emancipation Proclamation, declaring spiritual freedom. The confusing thing about being a spiritual person in terms of how the Bible defines it is that we don't have the option of having God's Spirit in us without living by it. We're told that not being led by the Spirit of God results in spiritual death. Because we're not delving into deep theological or philosophical discussion here, it's enough to suggest that anything other than relying on God's Spirit is detrimental to being a spiritual person. And, of course, it's detrimental to those who lead.

Spiritual leaders have an upper hand over non-spiritual leaders, in that they have access to insights and energy unique to the Spirit. Their ability to see what others can't, as well as to respond with greater faith, clarity, and boldness, raises their leading competence.

> *The man without the Spirit does not accept the things that come from the Spirit of God, for they are foolishness to him, and he cannot understand them, because they are spiritually discerned. The spiritual man makes judgments about all things, but he himself is not subject to any man's judgment: "For who has known the mind of the Lord that he may instruct him?" But we have the mind of Christ. (1 Corinthians 2:14-16)*

People who study history and religion often confuse past leaders who were moral and religious with spiritual leaders. The two concepts are complimentary, but not mutually inclusive. Spiritual people can go about leading from a non-spiritual mindset. Spiritual leadership requires people who are both spiritual and leaders, and who integrate how they rely on God with how they lead.

What's the Difference Between Spiritual Leaders and Religious Zealots?

To be both spiritual and a leader is a unique combination of values, life processes, motivations, and objectives. But being a spiritual person doesn't automatically make you a leader. At the same time, being a Christian who is a leader does not inevitably turn you into a spiritual leader. Too many Christian leaders divorce true spirituality from their leading roles. The result is that they practice the general form of leadership prevalent in the world.

Spiritual leaders rely on God, lead to serve, take risks out of faith rather than ego, and listen to the Spirit regarding timing, decisions, and relationship issues. In some ways, leading is no different from any other God-given gift: we are tempted to live life on our own, to take control, and to be the captains of our own souls.

This human predisposition makes spiritual leading even more difficult, because leaders by nature are take-charge people. Obviously, you can't influence when you're powerless. And transferring power and control to anyone else, deity or other, is antithetical to how leaders are wired. That's why true spiritual leaders are such a minority, because to become one, you must submit both personally and professionally to divine guidance and empowerment. Generic leaders may begin from a moral, spiritual vantage point. But they very quickly give up spiritual leading because it's foreign to them.

When our dependence on God's Spirit requires us to be silent, to appear incompetent, or to allow injustice to prevail beyond what we feel we can bear, the temptation to take charge can be overwhelming. "I'll do it myself" is as common among leaders as it is among parents who love their child but who find the child's inability to accomplish a task more than they can bear. Using our leading gifts on our own, apart from our Creator, is akin to using a pair of pliers to drive a nail. You may successfully drive the nail, but you're also apt to mess up more than if you'd have used an appropriate tool, because pliers were not created to pound nails.

Spiritual leaders shouldn't be confused with generic leaders who are self-righteous, overbearing, and autocratic Bible thumpers. When leaders become religious zealots, God gets bad PR and lousy marketing. The holy wars of the Middle Ages were far from what God desired in terms of Christian behavior. Tyrants in the pulpit and knuckle-rapping nuns don't reflect strong, spiritual leadership. Synthetic spirituality may look like the real thing, but it fails to perform. At the same time, generic leaders can make things happen, but they rarely look like Jesus in the process. As vinyl is to genuine leather, so is religious leading to spiritual leading. True spiritual leadership is marked by a prevailing attitude of humility, hope, and passion.

WANTED: SPIRITUAL LEADERS!

Because of the inherent conflicts between leading and being authentically spiritual, few genuine spiritual leaders exist. While the need for leaders who are spiritually motivated and empowered is significant, the friction points are numerous. The temptations of strong leaders and the process of leadership are often the opposite of what makes a person spiritual. Like oil and water, the two arenas don't always mix well. Leaders who desire to be spiritual must consciously fight the tendency to lead by their own power. If sincere leaders are aware of these points of contention, they can better allow God to grace their leading with his presence.

A Merging of Leadership & Spirituality

Can a leader be both strong and spiritual?

What's the single biggest problem among leaders who want to be spiritual?

Why does the Enemy target spiritual leaders with failure and discouragement?

How did Jesus develop the attitude of a servant leader?

What's love got to do with it?

CAN A LEADER BE BOTH STRONG AND SPIRITUAL?

Let's shatter a myth—the one that says spiritual people are mild-mannered, weak, flimsy, and passive.

In the epic movie *Ghandi*, the title character says, "I have never advocated passive anything; nonviolence, yes; passivity, no." The reputation of historical and contemporary leaders who are assertive as well as coercive and mean-spirited has conditioned us to believe that if you're going to be powerful, you must be manipulative and autocratic. But let's stop the myth; surliness isn't a prerequisite for effective leading. The inverse perception is that if you're not controlling, you are weak-kneed and easily swayed. Another myth down; "door-mat" leading has little to do with spiritual leading.

Given the human propensity to live out of our own strengths as opposed to relying on the Spirit, giving in to the dominate emotions of anger, revenge, control, and intimidation are symptomatic of non-spiritual leading.

Someone who can't control himself or herself shouldn't be entrusted with the charge of leading others. But the paradox of biblical spirituality is that this self-control is not self-induced. Rather, it's a direct result of the leader yielding his or her life to the guidance and empowerment of God's Spirit. In other words, self-discipline is a misnomer when applied to spiritual life. When we submit to the Spirit of God, our lives are somehow allowed to be filled with that Spirit. Yet he respects our free will and ability to choose, and therefore doesn't force himself on us like some sort of demonic possession or corporate hostile takeover. God isn't a bully, even though he is very strong and at times very clear on how we should live our lives.

Power is an important topic in the Bible.

> For the kingdom of God is not a matter of talk but of power. (1 Corinthians 4:20)

> So [the angel] said to me, "This is the word of the LORD . . . : 'Not by might nor by power, but by my Spirit,' says the LORD Almighty.'" (Zechariah 4:6)

> Jesus replied, "Are you not in error because you do not know the Scriptures or the power of God?" (Mark 12:24)

> May the God of hope fill you with all joy and peace as you trust in him, so that you may overflow with hope by the power of the Holy Spirit. (Romans 15:13)

Religious wimps—people who claim to know God and his Spirit but are forever coming up short—are a dime a dozen.

Scripture talks about them as "having a form of godliness but denying its power. Have nothing to do with them" (2 Timothy 3:5). These are just a few references to the concept of power.

Leaders deal in power. The Greek work for power (*dunamis*) is where we get the English words "dynamite" and "dynamic." When someone is dynamic, he or she exudes power. If you don't have power as a leader, you cease to lead. An impotent leader is an oxymoron. If you are uncomfortable with power to the point of avoiding it, you'll never rise to be a leader that God or anyone can use.

When Moses initially rejected God's request to lead his people out of Egypt, God became frustrated with him. People suffering from low self-esteem and false humility often shy away from power, sometimes to the applause of seemingly spiritual people who see such an attitude as an act of piety. This misunderstanding gets perpetuated in circles that don't recognize the importance of power both to lead and to perform the tasks that our Creator has designed for us. This sort of reaction is common as an overcompensation for power gone awry. Too many people have been hurt and ruined by power, so they shun it at all costs.

Electricity is a wonderful friend, but if we fail to respect it adequately, it can kill us. The same is true of power. The best guard against power gone awry is to nurture God's power. Human power is reckless and difficult to control. Spiritual power comes with a built-in governor to regulate it constructively.

The primary downside of any kind of power is its strong narcotic effect. Power can easily become addictive because it increases our ability to control circumstances. It gives us the feelings of self-control and self-sufficiency that are the substances of sin. Becoming our own god was the essence of the first sin and is the underlying component of every subsequent sin throughout history. But if you want to be a spiritual leader, you must be willing not only to dabble, but also to immerse yourself in the concept of power.

The big difference between human leading and spiritual leading is both the source and the nature of the power. Human-generated power is limited because of its source, and it therefore relies primarily on force, manipulation, human skill, position, money, and work ethic. Spiritual power may employ a few of these means as tools, but surpasses the realm of human leading. God has an uncanny ability to work behind the scenes and via ways invisible to the five senses.

> *"For my thoughts are not your thoughts, neither are your ways my ways," declares the LORD. "As the heavens are higher than the earth, so are my ways higher than your ways and my thoughts than your thoughts."* (Isaiah 55:8-9)

WHAT'S THE SINGLE BIGGEST PROBLEM AMONG LEADERS WHO WANT TO BE SPIRITUAL?

Again, leaders who want to be spiritual leaders must guard against relying on their own power and resources instead of God's. It's a natural temptation to want to call our own shots. The most confusing situation—particularly for followers and collaborators—is when we sincerely desire to do things for God but via our own ways and means. Well-intentioned people fail to understand that just as important as *what* we achieve is *how* we achieve.

When Gideon was faced with an enemy army, he initially did what any military leader would do: put together as many resources as possible and blow them away. But God had a different idea: "The LORD said to Gideon, 'You have too many men for me to deliver Midian into their hands. In order that Israel may not boast against me that her own strength has saved her . . .'" (Judges 7:2). As a result, the strategic plan changed from thirty-two thousand troops to three hundred.

What is ludicrous to humans is not out of the question when we're leading spiritually. Of course, this isn't to say that the ludicrous is proof of spirituality. Faith appears foolish at times, but fools aren't necessarily faithful. The inept who blame God for their guidance give the truly spiritual a bad name.

Jesus said, "Remain in me, and I will remain in you. No branch can bear fruit by itself; it must remain in the vine. Neither can you bear fruit unless you remain in me" (John 15:4). To be spiritual in a biblical sense means that the benefit we bring through our leading is an *eternal* benefit only if we plug into Jesus, the vine. While history is marked with the acts of good and bad influencers, these pale with what God deems as lasting fruit. Therefore, if we want our leading to make a significant difference in both mundane and sublime matters, we must work hard to do less on our own and more by relying on God.

The temptation to work out of our own gifting is persistent. Jesus said it is harder for a rich person to get into heaven than for a camel to crawl through a very tiny space. Wealth has to do with any resource above the norm or above what is required to survive. These resource crutches disable our spiritual acumen. When we rely on our God-given talents rather than on God's anointing, we poke holes in the leadership fabric, which weakens it. Spiritual leaders learn to fight the constant urge to do things themselves, understanding there is victory in surrender.

WHY DOES THE ENEMY TARGET SPIRITUAL LEADERS WITH FAILURE AND DISCOURAGEMENT?

If you buy into the biblical boundaries of the spiritual realm, you must address the possibility of a type of spiritual warfare that goes on behind the scenes and at times manifests itself in the lives of people.

For our struggle is not against flesh and blood, but
against the rulers, against the authorities, against the
powers of this dark world and against the spiritual
forces of evil in the heavenly realms. (Ephesians 6:12)

Your enemy the devil prowls around like a roaring lion
looking for someone to devour. (1 Peter 5:8)

Forget the Halloween costume version of the devil with
horns, pitchfork, red cape, and arrowhead tail. If we consider
the spiritual realm a reality, we must ponder the possibilities
of entities and influences that are invisible to our senses. The
Bible gives several examples of Jesus' interaction with these
evil spirits. He didn't deny their existence, but he didn't let
their presence intimidate him either. He confronted them con-
fidently and challenged them. He also didn't look at every
problem as a spiritual one or blame all mishaps on demonic
forces.

But assuming that a spiritual war does exist between the
forces of good and evil, it only makes sense that a prime target for spiritual attacks is leaders. In human warfare, strate-
gists know the importance of taking out the command posts,
leaders, and communication centers. Because leadership is a
social process in which a few individuals receive resources to
influence others, any competitive mindset will try to render
powerless those with the most influence.

Therefore, spiritual leaders are aware that they have a
bull's-eye on their forehead when it comes to the spiritual enemies of our Creator. When they step across the line of commitment, spiritual leaders walk into the crosshairs of
opposing gun sights. Spiritual people often don't know the
source of their challenges, whether they're organizational,
relational, or even spiritual. But they don't rule out the latter.
When a temptation comes, whether it be in the form of envy,
greed, sex, anger, revenge, or another, a leader can rarely iden-

tify whether it's an internally generated response to stress or fear of success, or it's an externally initiated attack from the Enemy. The key isn't so much to correctly identify the source as it is to be prepared. Smart spiritual leaders simply understand that circumstances arise that transcend human understanding and must be handled through spiritual means. In other words, you don't take out an incoming nuclear missile with a handgun. Spiritual weapons require spiritual defenses.

The solution is found in this passage:

> Be self-controlled and alert. Your enemy the devil prowls around like a roaring lion looking for someone to devour. Resist him, standing firm in the faith, because you know that your brothers throughout the world are undergoing the same kind of sufferings. (1 Peter 5:8-9)

This makes it clear that we're not to take spiritual opposition lightly. But we also don't need to be fearful of it.

For the novice spiritual leader, talk of this spiritual battle can seem both eerie and intimidating. It's much easier to pretend that it doesn't exist than to adequately prepare for spiritual attacks. Like so many governments have learned, you can't make the enemies go away just by pretending they don't exist. The key isn't to overprepare out of paranoia, just as we shouldn't underprepare out of ignorance or suppressed fear.

How Did Jesus Develop the Attitude of a Servant Leader?

> Do nothing out of selfish ambition or vain conceit, but in humility consider others better than yourselves. Each of you should look not only to your own interests, but also to the interests of others. Your attitude should

> *be the same as that of Christ Jesus: Who, being in very nature God, did not consider equality with God something to be grasped, but made himself nothing, taking the very nature of a servant, being made in human likeness. And being found in appearance as a man, he humbled himself and became obedient to death—even death on a cross! Therefore God exalted him to the highest place and gave him the name that is above every name. (Philippians 2:3-9)*

If Jesus is the ultimate model of spiritual leadership, we can learn a lot from this attitude-revealing passage. After he told his leadership protégés to become least if they wanted to become great, Jesus practiced what he preached. The result of Jesus humbling himself—even experiencing death on the cross—was that God exalted him to the highest place. Jesus consistently practiced giving up his rights.

Because of their power and position, leaders usually have more "rights" than anyone. Unfortunately, these rights also wreak havoc with our souls. Entitlements can make us lazy, self-centered, or stingy. Spiritual leaders are not coerced to surrender these rights, but voluntarily practice the habit.

According to this passage, the first right Jesus gave up was a most basic human right: the right to be himself. Jesus was by nature God. His DNA was the same as his heavenly Father's, but he didn't claim the rights he deserved as the possessor of this quality.

Think about how many times we justify our insensitive, self-centered behaviors: "That's just the way I am." "I'm an only child." "I'm a middle child." "I'm a redhead." "I had harsh potty training." "I'm from a dysfunctional family." "I _____" (fill in your favorite). These kinds of blanket comments don't give us license to be jerks. At best, they may help others understand why sometimes we're jerk-like. But surrendering our right to be ourselves is one of the qualities of servanthood. This is a position of ultimate power—overcoming ourselves. Spiritual leaders understand that unless they're able to implement self-denial, they'll never realize their full potential at leading. Submitting to God's power is voluntary. He doesn't overpower us with a possessive sort of control. Only as we learn to surrender our most basic right of expressing ourselves can we hope to let his Spirit flow through us.

Jesus also surrendered his right to be respected. Instead of being born in a palace of a royal family and riding into his kingdom on a white stallion, Jesus took the back door, slipping in where few noticed him. Obviously, Jesus wanted people to know that he was the Son of God, but he wasn't consumed with wielding power.

Spiritual leaders aren't overly concerned about their ranking, applause, or standing in the polls. When leaders invest too much energy in self-promotion or recognition-grooming, they limit their ultimate benefit to an organization. Spiritual leaders understand that long-term respect doesn't come from a position, title, office size, reserved parking spot, or front-row seat. They're able to sneak in the back, wash some feet, make some sacrifices, and as a result have a profound impact on other people's lives. Dispersing credit to fellow team members and sharing the spotlight is a clear characteristic of servanthood.

Finally, Jesus surrendered his right to win. He became obedient to death, even death on a cross. As the Creator of life, he had the power to live forever and to save himself from the disgusting, unjustified humiliation of the Crucifixion. But he submitted to God's ultimate will. Without Jesus' death, there wouldn't have been any plan for salvation. If he had saved himself, he would have lost present and future followers.

Leaders tend to be competitive, and most enjoy a good win. It makes no human sense to lose when you have the capabilities to win. But leaders also know that sometimes winning means losing. Winning an argument can mean the loss of a relationship. Winning a battle can result in losing a war.

Winning self-esteem can cost the allegiance of followers. Winning an immediate goal can leave you short of a long-term objective. If leaders don't learn the discipline of giving up the right to win, they'll fail to benefit their followers.

Philippians 2:3-9, where we see Jesus' sacrifice of his rights, is called the *kenosis* passage—which means "giving up" or "emptying." Leading is about obtaining power, accumulating influence. But leadership changes when it intersects with spirituality. Then leadership includes strategically giving up human elements in order to obtain spiritual ones. The ability to do this has a lot to do with self-image.

We can see Jesus' security and identity in his premier demonstration of servant leadership:

> *Jesus knew that the Father had put all things under his power, and that he had come from God and was returning to God; so he got up from the meal, took off his outer clothing, and wrapped a towel around his waist. After that, he poured water into a basin and began to wash his disciples' feet, drying them with the towel that was wrapped around him. . . .*
>
> *When he had finished washing their feet, he put on his clothes and returned to his place. "Do you understand what I have done for you?" he asked them. "You call me 'Teacher' and 'Lord,' and rightly so, for that is what I am. Now that I, your Lord and Teacher, have washed your feet, you also should wash one another's feet. I have set you an example that you should do as I have done for you. I tell you the truth, no servant is greater than his master, nor is a messenger greater than the one who sent him. Now that you know these things, you will be blessed if you do them." (John 13:3-5,12-17)*

The closer we get to understanding that our power as spiritual leaders comes from God, the more secure we'll be, allowing us to fulfill servant roles as leaders. Conversely, the less secure we are about our position, our calling, and our destination, the less likely we'll be humble at tasks as leaders. When a leader is insecure in his or her position, power, and self-esteem, service will be limited.

What's Love Got to Do with It?

Remember the intersection of Gurley and Montezuma streets that we used as a metaphor for describing where leadership and spirituality intersect? You'll also find spiritual leadership where love and strength overlap. Non-spiritual leadership often lies beyond this intersection, where you find the negative symptoms of power: coercion, manipulation, intimidation by anger, autocracy, threat, and inflated egos.

You can help determine whether or not you're leading primarily from a spiritual power base by analyzing the relational climate of your group or organization. Remember that leadership is about people working together toward mutual outcomes. So measuring the characteristics of your relationships is much like an investigator analyzing DNA.

> The fruit of the Spirit is love, joy, peace, patience, kindness, goodness, faithfulness, gentleness and self-control. Against such things there is no law. Those who belong to Christ Jesus have crucified the sinful nature with its passions and desires. Since we live by the Spirit, let us keep in step with the Spirit. (Galatians 5:22-25)

If the characteristics described in these verses are prevalent, chances are good that God is present. At a non-spiritual leadership crime scene, these traces are missing.

But be sure these characteristics are authentic. For example, mushy sentimentality is a poor substitute for genuine love. Don't accept counterfeits.

Love is patient, love is kind. It does not envy, it does not boast, it is not proud. It is not rude, it is not self-seeking, it is not easily angered, it keeps no record of wrongs. Love does not delight in evil but rejoices with the truth. It always protects, always trusts, always hopes, always perseveres. Love never fails. (1 Corinthians 13:4-8)

The best kind of love is tough and tenacious. It doesn't put up with flimsy excuses or self-destructive behavior. Love seeks what is best for people. Looking out for the welfare of others is the ultimate role of a leader. Self-centered leading is a sham and nothing short of organizational embezzlement and misappropriation of resources. Leadership wasn't created for the benefit of those who lead. Spiritual leaders are servants. If leaders benefit from leading, so be it. But if they don't benefit, true spiritual leaders will lead anyway.

Spiritual leaders who function by the Holy Spirit emanate love, for God is love. Scripture repeatedly makes this clear:

Dear friends, let us love one another, for love comes from God. Everyone who loves has been born of God and knows God. Whoever does not love does not know God, because God is love. (1 John 4:7-8)

And so we know and rely on the love God has for us. God is love. Whoever lives in love lives in God, and God in him. (1 John 4:16)

If I speak in the tongues of men and of angels, but have not love, I am only a resounding gong or a clanging cymbal. If I have the gift of prophecy and can fathom all mysteries and all knowledge, and if I have a faith that can move mountains, but have not love, I am nothing. If I give all I possess to the poor and surrender my body to the flames, but have not love, I gain nothing. (1 Corinthians 13:1-3)

The die is cut for us to continue this truth by saying, "If I exude incredible leader abilities and help my organization achieve great things, but do not have love, I have failed."

It's clear that spiritual leaders can never excuse their unloving behaviors by saying, "I can't love well; I'm the leader." Strength and love are not mutually exclusive. Maintaining the precarious balance between strength and love over the long haul is impossible without the prevailing power that only comes from God. Spiritual leaders must graciously and wisely weave together power and grace, strength and love, never excluding one from the other.

If I exude incredible leader abilities and help my organization achieve great things, but do not have love, I have failed as a spiritual leader.

A Spiritual Leader's Inner Life

What kind of self-perception should spiritual leaders have?

How does a spiritual leader deal with ego?

What part does prayer play in a spiritual leader's life?

Why is it so hard for spiritual leaders to pray?

How do the prayers of spiritual leaders differ from those of non-leaders?

Why do spiritual leaders have a hard time developing personal support?

Why does it seem that so many spiritual leaders struggle in the area of sexual temptation?

How can spiritual leaders avoid misusing sexual energy?

How can spiritual leaders avoid other temptations of leadership?

How much Christian community should be on a spiritual leader's schedule?

How much personal time with God should be on a spiritual leader's schedule?

WHAT KIND OF SELF-PERCEPTION SHOULD SPIRITUAL LEADERS HAVE?

Maxwell Maltz, plastic surgeon turned author/psychologist, discovered that when he surgically enhanced the appearance of his patients, sometimes they still looked in the mirror and saw a deformed person. He realized that we often respond not to how we actually are or even how others see us; instead we respond to how we see ourselves.

Your self-image is how you perceive yourself. And how we see ourselves is a strong determiner of how we respond to people and situations. The same is true of leaders. A leader with a good self-image will likely respond differently to circumstances than one with a poor self-image. The self-image of a leader has a lot to do with strengths and weaknesses in leading. And spirituality has a significant impact on self-perception.

Leaders who are spiritually mature will demonstrate a significant amount of servant leadership. This kind of leading comes from a humble heart that's in tune with its Creator as well as its purpose among other creations. Although I know a few people who seem only marginally spiritual and yet portray a servant's attitude, I'm not sure how deep this disposition can truly go without roots in the soul. By far, most of the people I know who want to display and maintain a servant's heart need the kind of character growth that only comes through spiritual means. This is especially true among those of us wired to lead.

Most of us with leadership gifts or who are in leader roles naturally develop the self-image of a leader. People look to us to take charge. "Where's the leader?" "Are you leading here?" "I'd like to talk to the leader."

Most of us in service organizations would describe our leading as a way to serve others. The problem is, this doesn't go far enough, because we need to see ourselves first and foremost as servants. Servants use whatever they have at their disposal to serve others. Sometimes it's a towel and basin. Or it might be cooking. Still other times servants cut hair, mow yards, answer phones, change diapers, manage businesses, sell, teach, coach, drive cars, or do secretarial work.

Spiritual leaders see themselves primarily as servants, not leaders. Leading is merely a tool God has entrusted with us to use as a vehicle to serve others.

A friend of mine, Terry Bassett, owns and operates an auto repair garage. On the days my car needs servicing, I drive my car down to his business and drop it off. His auto technicians all wear the same uniforms and have their own tools. Sometimes my car needs an oil change, sometimes new brake pads. And still other days, the air conditioning needs to be charged. Different mechanics may do different jobs: one assists customers while another does oil changes. Regardless of the tasks, the basic job title is "auto technician." Their identity and their uniform fit their role, no matter what the specific tasks at hand are.

In God's plan, everyone wears the same uniform, because everyone holds the same position—servant. If we have this attitude, then when we're not leading we maintain our identity; we don't think of ourselves as leaders but as servants. Servant leaders are servants who merely use leading as a tool for serving others.

How Does a Spiritual Leader Deal with Ego?

Since the advent of psychology after the turn of the century, there's been a lot of confusion regarding the concept of ego and its integration with theology. To some, psychology has become a sort of theology, where the study of human nature has supplanted worship of God. On the other hand, some Christian circles have all but labeled psychological thought mumbo jumbo.

If all truth is God's truth, then we don't need to fear truth even if it lies outside of direct biblical teachings. Some truths simply help us understand the complexities and beauty of how God created us and the universe. The word "ego" has to do with who we are as people—our core nature, or our selves. Ego has to do with our identity. It represents our very existence. The Bible never tells us to get rid of our ego, even though some might suggest it does. To get rid of the ego would be like committing suicide. Jesus had an ego, an identity, a self. We're not to get rid of the ego or self, just the old nature within our personhood.

For we know that our old self was crucified with him so that the body of sin might be done away with, that we should no longer be slaves to sin. (Romans 6:6)

You were taught, with regard to your former way of life, to put off your old self, which is being corrupted by its deceitful desires; to be made new in the attitude of your minds; and to put on the new self, created to be like God in true righteousness and holiness. (Ephesians 4:22-24)

Do not lie to each other, since you have taken off your old self with its practices and have put on the new self, which is being renewed in knowledge in the image of its Creator. (Colossians 3:9-10)

A spiritual leader must have a strong sense of identity to lead well. And finding that value and identity in God through Christ is the best way to avoid human motivations. Only through spiritual means can the impurities of the old nature within be removed.

Am I now trying to win the approval of men, or of God? Or am I trying to please men? If I were still trying to please men, I would not be a servant of Christ. (Galatians 1:10)

Spiritual leaders choose God as boss. As a result, they are less bound by the goals and expectations of others. I use the word "less" because as humans, we are always influenced by others, whether they're peers, family members, parents, siblings, friends, or others in our organizations. Leaders who are fully unencumbered by the influence of others are dangerous. But our goal is not to be a puppet to other people. When Pinocchio came to life and could move without strings, he was still manipulated by the invisible strings of negative peers. We don't serve in order to please others, to win commitment, to make them like us, or for later payback. Instead, we have a single boss—Christ. We serve others by leading them, as an expression of serving Christ.

> *Submit to one another out of reverence for Christ.* (*Ephesians 5:21*)

Our ego is a vital part of our spirituality. It accounts for our self-image, how we perceive ourselves. Ego is doubly important in a leader's life because of this person's influence. When an ego is maligned, misperceived, or maladjusted, the ramifications within the organization are significant. On the positive side, healthy leader egos are huge benefits to an organization.

Ego size. The size of a leader's ego has to do with whether or not that person is willing and able to deny his or her desire for ego feeding. Just as people overeat and become obese, people with inflated egos tend to gorge themselves with ego food (attention, control, rewards, limelight).

Many leaders would do well to wear a sign around their neck: "Please don't feed the ego." A large ego is prideful, boastful, and self-centered. A large ego can be a difficult force to handle, and it works against becoming a truly spiritual leader.

A small ego is equivalent to true humility. Because it is able to surrender its desires, it doesn't overeat. The challenge of maintaining a small ego varies from person to person and situation to situation. Just as some people have metabolisms that let them eat anything and stay slim, some leaders maintain a small ego in spite of huge accolades. On the other hand, some seem to overdose on even the smallest amount of praise, power, and attention. And then they yearn for more. A person's disposition depends on temperament, early conditioning, and brokenness. In fact, brokenness is God's prime tool for ego pruning.

Ego strength. As opposed to ego size, ego *strength* has to do with self-esteem. This pertains to our sense of value. A weak ego is a sign of low self-esteem. A strong ego is a sign of high self-esteem. Leaders need a certain level of self-esteem to avoid being the pawns of followers and competing influencers. This is also how they can withstand the conflict of change and develop the tough hide that they sometimes need for strong leading.

The idea of self-esteem has also taken a hit in certain religious circles. But self-esteem comes from recognizing God's love for us. Spiritually grounded self-esteem anchors its value on being made in the image of God.

> *So God created man in his own image, in the image of God he created him; male and female he created them.* (Genesis 1:27)

Moses forgot this when he tried to avoid a leadership position that God was calling him to:

> *Moses said to the LORD, "O Lord, I have never been eloquent, neither in the past nor since you have spoken to your servant. I am slow of speech and tongue." The LORD said to him, "Who gave man his mouth? Who makes him deaf or mute? Who gives him sight or makes him blind? Is it not I, the LORD?" (Exodus 4:10-11)*

A healthy ego doesn't slight the abilities or innate value God has given us. And neither does it consume more calories than it can adequately digest without gaining weight.

Small, strong ego: This is the goal of the servant leader— the strong, loving leader. Appropriateness is the key. When it's time to "clear the temple," ego strength allows a leader to make the tough calls. At any given moment, people may confuse ego strength with ego size. But strong egos aren't necessarily big ones. Remember, Jesus had the same ego when he overturned the money changers' tables and when he washed the dirty feet of subordinates. Anonymity and acts of service done without fanfare are signs of a humble heart. Humble strength is usually the sign of a spiritual leader—a person who has the inner strength that comes from being in tune with his or her God-given value, as well as the security that allows the person to take submissive roles when appropriate.

The leader with a strong, small ego is the one who people love to follow. Leading becomes an act of service as opposed to an extension of the leader's identity. A servant leader doesn't base his or her identity on the gift or act of leading. Servant leaders see themselves as servants who can use any number of available tools for serving. When leading is available and necessary, these servants pick up the leader tool and use it with confidence. Leaders create a healthy leadership environment when they don't drain the organization of energy in order to feed their ego appetite. Twenty-first-century leading is about modeling service as well as creating a culture where serving others is the norm rather than the exception. Leaders initiate this example. They advocate, reward, and above all *model* servant actions and attitudes to foster a follower-friendly organization that engages people toward constructive action.

Spiritual and psychological integration is essential at this point. Non-spiritual people overemphasize the importance of emotional maturity. Overly spiritual people assume that seeking God alone is sufficient to overcome any emotional barrier. Spiritual leaders realize that God has made us as whole, complex people. The aspects of our personhood interact with each other for better and worse. Spiritual growth can be hindered by mental or emotional barriers. A number of processes tend to make us into the people we are. Some of these are voluntary;

others are involuntary. The big difference is in how we respond to what happens to us.

This is why some people emerge stronger through difficult challenges while others shrivel. This is where spirituality makes a difference. When we trust God and relinquish control over unanswered questions or past injustices and failures, we allow the conditions to tenderize our souls and we avoid potential emotional blockages that impede the Spirit's movement. Emotional hurts are akin to cholesterol in the heart, which can clog our arteries, leading to heart disease. When we disallow the healing presence of the Spirit in certain areas of our lives, we run the risk of being the walking wounded. Spiritual leadership is not just about ego strength or spiritual maturity. It is about both. The result is strong, loving leadership that maximizes a group's potential because its people are led well by a genuine servant.

What Part Does Prayer Play in a Spiritual Leader's Life?

Spiritual leaders rely heavily on the power of prayer. Prayer is the primary connection that allows us to receive God's Spirit, which enables us to be spiritual. It's akin to filling your car with gas.

The challenge of prayer for leaders is that people who are gifted at leading tend to find the process of being still before God a torturous one. They would rather just do something and hope that God blesses it. Leaders tend to be go-getters who are tempted to rely on their own gifting. As a result, most spiritual leaders have to work hard at their prayer life, constantly governing their desire to act before spending adequate time in prayer.

"I [Jesus] pray for them [the disciples]. I am not praying for the world, but for those you have given me, for they

*are yours. All I have is yours, and all you have is mine.
And glory has come to me through them. I will remain in
the world no longer, but they are still in the world, and I
am coming to you. Holy Father, protect them by the
power of your name—the name you gave me—so that
they may be one as we are one. While I was with them, I
protected them and kept them safe by that name you gave
me. None has been lost except the one doomed to destruction so that Scripture would be fulfilled. . . .*

*"My prayer is not that you take them out of the world
but that you protect them from the evil one. They are not
of the world, even as I am not of it. Sanctify them by the
truth; your word is truth. As you sent me into the world,
I have sent them into the world. For them I sanctify
myself, that they too may be truly sanctified.*

*"My prayer is not for them alone. I pray also for those
who will believe in me through their message, that all of
them may be one, Father, just as you are in me and I am
in you. May they also be in us so that the world may
believe that you have sent me." (John 17:9-12,15-21)*

From this model prayer, we learn three things about a spiritual leader's prayers. First, spiritual leaders pray for their teammates. They lift them up to God and commit them to his care.
Human leaders try on their own to groom their followers but
often end up irritated with and critical of the very people they
need help from to accomplish their goals. But how many of
these leaders invest in prayer time for their collaborators and
followers? Personal and professional intercession goes a long
way in changing both the follower and the leader. Asking God
to intervene and to help the people working for you or serving
under you will temper what you say and how you say it.

Second, spiritual leaders pray for themselves to be good
leaders and providers for their team and organization. Jesus
said that he had preserved the disciples when they were under

his care. This kind of prayer presents the leader as a servant to the followers. An emotional role spiritual leaders fulfill is that of a shepherd and chaplain. The leader is a pastor and the organization is his or her parish. Followers don't exist to please the leader; the leader exists to help them reach their potential within the organization.

Third, spiritual leaders pray for the end users, the customers and benefactors of the organization. Jesus prayed for the people who would eventually be affected by the influence of his disciples. People shouldn't be used to make an organization rich. When headed by a spiritual leader, an organization—even if it turns a profit—should have the primary goal of benefiting society and serving people. This perspective creates a service mindset in a leader.

Model prayer: In the book of 2 Chronicles, Jehoshaphat provides an example of prayer for spiritual leaders to follow:

> *The Moabites and Ammonites with some of the Meunites came to make war on Jehoshaphat. Some men came and told Jehoshaphat, "A vast army is coming against you from Edom, from the other side of the Sea. It is already in Hazazon Tamar" (that is, En Gedi). Alarmed, Jehoshaphat resolved to inquire of the* LORD, *and he proclaimed a fast for all Judah.*
>
> *The people of Judah came together to seek help from the* LORD; *indeed, they came from every town in Judah to seek him. Then Jehoshaphat stood up in the assembly of Judah and Jerusalem at the temple of the* LORD *in the front of the new courtyard. (2 Chronicles 20:1-5)*

Human leaders who are spiritual but who rely on their own leadership skills tend to make their own plan and ask God to bless it. They strategize on their residual spiritual power, human wisdom, or past experience, and they finally resort to prayer only when things go awry.

But like Jehoshaphat, true spiritual leaders pray as a first response instead of as a last resort. Spiritual leaders begin with prayer. Jehoshaphat was confronted by a foreign army poised for attack. He didn't circle the wagons, pull out the artillery, or run to the hills. In what might seem odd to any worldly warrior, his first action of battle was to engage God.

When time is of the essence, prayer is not wasted effort. Spiritual leaders go to God first, knowing that their best chance for long-term success is to discover God's will.

Jehoshaphat also models a public stance in prayer. He didn't seek the privacy of his closet. He clearly went public with his spiritual dependence on God. While our different organizational cultures may limit our ability to be overt with our faith, a duty of spiritual leaders is to point people toward prayer.

We are told that "Jehoshaphat stood up in the assembly." We are sometimes fearful of doing this because we think we may appear incompetent because we don't have the answers ourselves. Or maybe we don't go public because we don't want to be held accountable for carrying out God's plans. Also, if people know we're spiritual leaders, then we'll have to prove it with the way we treat others. We'll need to take the high road regarding ethics and simply "practice what we preach."

So, we keep our prayer in the closet, thinking, "No one needs to know. I'll lead invisibly, like the wind, avoiding the attention that will come if people know I pray as a leader." As a spiritual leader, you'll have to make the call in each situation. But consider how a gentle, non-pushy comment regarding taking organizational issues to God might rally the troops.

Spiritual leaders are willing to wrestle with God for both organizational blessings and solutions to problems. They recognize that without the blessing of God, success may not be possible. If they do obtain success without God's blessing, it won't be fulfilling or enduring.

Leaders carry the emotional burden for their organization. They see the big picture better than anyone. They desire the organization to succeed more than anyone. This kind of burden, translated spiritually, results in wrestling with God from time to time. In the wee hours, when everyone else is asleep, spiritual leaders sometimes tug and pull at God for his touch.

WHY IS IT SO HARD FOR SPIRITUAL LEADERS TO PRAY?

The decision not to pray for God's desires reveals that a leader's priorities are out of sequence. It's not that we don't value God or soul growth. The error is that we let other things take priority over God, and we squeeze out the things that don't scream for our attention. Time restraints and overcommitments are perhaps the most pressing issues behind why we do not pray more. Three things stand out as the reasons leaders don't pray for the situations they're in as leaders.

1. *Leaders tend to be self-reliant and action oriented.* We've mentioned this before, but we need to say it again. The primary force working against the spiritual development of leaders is that by nature they are self-reliant. Self-motivation, confidence in their gifts, and a take-charge, go-get-'em attitude is what most leaders naturally have. Yet these God-given qualities ironically work against leaders' reliance on God.

> *The disciples were amazed at his words. But Jesus said again, "Children, how hard it is to enter the kingdom of God! It is easier for a camel to go through the eye of a needle than for a rich man to enter the kingdom of God." The disciples were even more amazed, and said to each other, "Who then can be saved?" (Mark 10:24-26)*

Wealth here is not just a matter of money. Sometimes rich people are those who simply have resources that seem to support them with little to no involvement by God. Talent, money, information, network, experience, sheer strength, and tenacity can be tools both for victory and for defeat. In this passage, the disciples were somewhat amazed with Jesus' words and asked, "Who then can be saved?" The popular idea of the day was that wealth and blessings were evidence of God's favor. The disciples didn't realize that resources weren't necessarily indicators of spirituality. They assumed, as we still do sometimes, that God-given gifts are equivalent to God-given anointing.

Most leaders are also doers by nature. When they see something undone, they want to fix it. They're organizational fixers, problem solvers, people of action. A strong indicator of a leader is one who demonstrates initiative.

> Be still before the LORD and wait patiently for him; do not fret when men succeed in their ways, when they carry out their wicked schemes. (Psalm 37:7)

"Wait patiently? You've got to be kidding! Do you know who I am? Do you know how important my job is? Do you know how many people are depending on me to be decisive and take action? I can't wait patiently. What will they think? I'll be accused of shirking my duty, sleeping at my post, or worse, of being lazy or incompetent. Doesn't action reflect courage and competence? What if we lose this window of opportunity? I don't get paid to wait. Others wait for me." This kind of self-talk inundates us as leaders, especially in an era of compressed time and decision making on the fly.

Personal initiative often works against being still and knowing God (Psalm 46:10). Throughout history, leaders who have substituted patience with action have had regrets. Abram conceived a child with Hagar instead of with his wife, resulting in Arab-Israeli tension even today (Genesis 16). Esau traded his birthright to Jacob (Genesis 25:29-34). Moses struck the rock instead of speaking to it (Numbers 20:8-12). King Saul couldn't wait for a priest to show up, so he made a sacrifice himself (1 Samuel 13:8-14). Peter pledged allegiance, yet slept during prayer time (Matthew 26:38-40). He then cut off a servant's ear instead of turning to Jesus for instructions (John 18:10-11).

Don't laugh at these spiritual buffoons. Most of us are wired the same way!

As leaders, our minds are often preoccupied with organizational noises. We take in all kinds of complex information and process it toward a preferred course of action. But the clamor of whirring thoughts from within the decision factory can keep us from hearing what needs to be heard—God's Spirit. Unfortunately, God rarely turns up his volume. He wants us to listen more carefully. Therefore, if we are to hear God, we must turn down our own volume.

> The LORD said, "Go out and stand on the mountain in the presence of the LORD, for the LORD is about to pass by." Then a great and powerful wind tore the mountains apart and shattered the rocks before the LORD, but the LORD was not in the wind. After the wind there was an earthquake, but the LORD was not in the earthquake. After the earthquake came a fire, but the LORD was not in the fire. And after the fire came a gentle whisper. (1 Kings 19:11-12)

Why does God whisper sometimes? Perhaps to force us to turn our attention to him. While we're busy seeking solutions, God seeks our presence. If he yelled, we wouldn't need to get close to him—we could lead from a distance. But God doesn't shout his instructions. He calls us into a holy huddle and then softly speaks what we need to hear. If we try to listen from too far away, we're apt to misunderstand the instructions and take the wrong road. So many words sound alike when our attention is distracted by the ambient noise that drifts into unfocused communication with God.

2. *Leaders tend to have many demands on their time.* Even when a leader delegates well, the requirements of decision making, innovation, change, and troubleshooting can easily deter the most sincere spiritual person. There's always something to do, it seems, when you're leading a dynamic organization: meetings to attend, staff and volunteers to deal with, papers to push, calls to return, and decisions to be made. When we're not firefighting, we're strategically planning controlled burns for the future. And besides work responsibilities, we have to wear the hats of husband/wife, father/mother, community volunteer, shopper, home fixer, home manager, and friend.

At the same time, the pace of twenty-first-century living has skyrocketed. Average workweeks have expanded. The tendency to do more faster is addictive and even required because of accelerated competition. It's no longer survival of the fittest; "survival of the fastest" is the new evolutionary slogan. Rapidity allows us more time to do more, so the speed never decelerates. Carving prayer time into a bulging schedule seems less like a pleasant option and more like a survival skill. The tyranny of the urgent becomes the *modus operandi* for most of us these days, resulting in shrunken souls and anemic spirituality.

3. *Leaders have the unique challenge of developing adequate, effective accountability.* At a leadership conference, participants were instructed to write down what they thought was the percentage of energy and time a leader should invest in leading up (those over you), leading down (those under you), leading laterally (team members), and leading inwardly (developing yourself as a leader).

When attendees were finished guessing, the speaker revealed the advice of one leadership guru. Gasps were heard across the auditorium when he stated that the most effective leadership balance was 10 percent on lateral leading, 20 percent on leading down, 20 percent on leading up, and 50

percent on inner development. In other words, the most effective leaders invest significant time and energy making sure
that the "ax is sharp"—that they are well read and that their
mind, body, and soul are at their best. When the inner leader
becomes depleted, it adversely affects everything the leader
touches. When the inner leader is nourished, the entire organization benefits.[1]

HOW DO THE PRAYERS OF SPIRITUAL LEADERS DIFFER FROM THOSE OF NON-LEADERS?

Of course, the work of prayer is difficult in and of itself.
Though leaders seem to have the deck stacked against them,
they do have a few things in their favor that should allow
them to make prayer a habit.

1. *No one knows the big picture as well as the leader.* In terms
of praises and requests, leaders are privy to both macro and
micro organizational issues. Who better to bring the organization to God than its leader? No one can articulate the needs
and culture better than the leader. When available, specificity
is an integral part of prayer. The ability to articulate problems
and needed outcomes is best suited for the person with the
best view. The leader can pray more strategically, understanding people, circumstances, and details as no one else can.
Using this knowledge for effective prayer allows the leader to
have both a long and an accurate list of what needs to happen.

2. *No one feels the burden more than the leader.* No one
should be more passionate about helping the organization
succeed than its leader. This may be the single strongest influence driving a leader to prayer.

> *Then Jesus went with his disciples to a place called
> Gethsemane, and he said to them, "Sit here while I go
> over there and pray." He took Peter and the two sons of
> Zebedee along with him, and he began to be sorrowful*

and troubled. Then he said to them, "My soul is over-whelmed with sorrow to the point of death. Stay here and keep watch with me."

Going a little farther, he fell with his face to the ground and prayed, "My Father, if it is possible, may this cup be taken from me. Yet not as I will, but as you will."

Then he returned to his disciples and found them sleeping. "Could you men not keep watch with me for one hour?" he asked Peter. "Watch and pray so that you will not fall into temptation. The spirit is willing, but the body is weak."

He went away a second time and prayed, "My Father, if it is not possible for this cup to be taken away unless I drink it, may your will be done." When he came back, he again found them sleeping, because their eyes were heavy. So he left them and went away once more and prayed the third time. (Matthew 26:36-44)

Leading can be painful as well as joyful. The weight of leading can prompt leaders to pray so that they're not over-whelmed or overly anxious. Dumping on God is therapeutic both for leaders and for the organizations they lead. When leaders get too close to the organization, the sheer stress can create problems.

Cast all your anxiety on him because he cares for you.
(1 Peter 5:7)

While a certain level of stress helps us reach our potential, too much stress shakes us to pieces. To maintain a proper state of mind, a leader needs to let go of the stress that the pressures of leading create. Spiritual leaders can turn this potentially negative energy into positive if they let it drive them to prayer. Countless leaders in the Bible turned their burdens into motivation for seeking God.

3. *No one has greater responsibility than the leader.* As a leader, your responsibility is to help your organization succeed and reach its potential. One of the ways to do this is through your connection with God. Your job is to do your best to make choices that will benefit the organization most. A part of your job is to pray, so that you call upon the power and wisdom of God.

If you're not praying, you're not doing your job! If you're not praying, you're less than what you need to be for others. They're depending on you. Prayer helps you be at your best. Prayer isn't pulling away from your work; it's part of your work.

Because prayer is the way you tap into the supernatural power and guidance of the Spirit, you're much less of a leader when you don't pray. Busying yourself with action makes you feel like you're doing your job. If people catch you meditating, kneeling in solitude, or being quiet in your office, they may accuse you of inaction. Ironically, this game is nearly always played in your mind, not in reality. Rest assured that most of your team would appreciate your seeking God's clear direction in your decision making and relationships. They'll applaud your search for wisdom beyond yourself.

Because you're the most important person within your area of responsibility, it's your utmost duty to maximize your potential. That's what prayer is about.

WHY DO SPIRITUAL LEADERS HAVE A HARD TIME DEVELOPING PERSONAL SUPPORT?

Remember that spiritual leaders aren't necessarily leaders of spiritually oriented organizations. Some spiritual leaders find themselves in cultures where their peers seldom talk about God. Prayer might be considered unimportant to other team members. This leaves the spiritual leader alone in his or her efforts to be disciplined in prayer. Developing prayer support within a non-spiritual organization can be troublesome because of the political dynamic of showing up for prayer led by "the boss." Prayer can also be less honest when it becomes a gossip center for personal and professional challenges. When a leader shares personal requests among subordinates or superiors, the human nature of judging can adversely impact the person praying.

Leaders within spiritually oriented communities find other factors to fight. For example, we often talk about prayer more than we actually pray. This is similar to a dieting support group talking about exercise and nutrition as they sit around a table loaded with munchies. Spiritual talk can often replace spiritual practices, and we deceive ourselves into believing that our talk is doing good.

Leaders can damage their leading by verbalizing fears and weaknesses. You can't undo certain revelations. For a leader, confessing sins in front of others is healthy only to a point. While a certain level of honesty and vulnerability allows people to relate to you, too much openness works the opposite way. Followers may appreciate your humanity, but if you are too transparent, their respect for you as a leader decreases. Losing credibility can drain trust in your leadership and may lessen your level of influence. This could leave you alone in some of your most challenging times.

An alternative is to develop prayer accountability among peers. This becomes challenging because of the time demands other leaders face. Finding common and consistent prayer times within multiple leaders' calendars can be very challenging. And if you have too few times together, you won't be able to establish adequate levels of trust and vulnerability; as a result, prayers and confessions will lack depth and intimacy. In addition, leaders may view each other as competitors and therefore find it difficult to be open or to share weaknesses. And finally, the mobility of the culture works against longevity, meaning that leaders don't always develop significant relationships, for fear that they will be short-term and shallow.

Spiritual leaders would do well to organize prayer chains and support groups whenever they can. But unlike other organizational work, prayer can't be delegated. Spiritual leaders can't assign the task to more spiritually-oriented associates. They must convince themselves that a very important part of their duty is to pray regularly. The purpose is twofold: First, it is to invest the time necessary for prayer to change the leader so that he or she is truly a *spiritual* leader. This means spending suitable chunks of time in Scripture reading, meditation, prayer, and solitude. Second, regular prayer allows the leader to hear from God regarding organizational issues. Praying for team members and challenges and opportunities within the organization demonstrates a reliance on God. Certain solutions and changed circumstances only come via spiritual processes that prayer stimulates.

Community ministerial associations have existed for some time. Many aren't designed to provide personal support for those involved. I'm a part of a group called Pastors In Covenant, which meets monthly for about two to three hours, just to "touch base." Mostly it is a friendship group. There are pastors from congregations of various sizes. We go on an annual retreat, pray, and share both shallow and deep personal and professional concerns. E-mails connect us between meetings, as do one-on-one lunches as desired. Anyone is free to set the agenda, using the group for accountability, feedback, and wisdom. Groups like this can work in both church and business sectors, providing a unique blend of personal and professional support.

WHY DOES IT SEEM THAT SO MANY SPIRITUAL LEADERS STRUGGLE IN THE AREA OF SEXUAL TEMPTATION?

For some people, the terms "spirituality" and "sexuality" are opposites. But because spirituality is a core issue and affects everything about us—both public and private—its impact upon our sexuality is significant.

Leaders are perceived as social role models. We look to them as examples of how we should behave and think. Whether they like it or not, their influence sets trends, validates actions, or revokes values. That's why leaders need to be especially careful in how they express themselves sexually, because their role in society plays a significant part in establishing how the rest of us deal with our own sexuality.

The two most common reasons for leader dropout seem to be discouragement/burnout and sexual infidelity. Sometimes the two are related. We shouldn't be surprised that our spiritual enemy would attack leaders most in these two vulnerable areas. As I've stated throughout this book, the reason leaders need spiritual power is because when they fail, it adversely affects many people. When a regular person fails in the sexual area, the impact is potentially devastating, but on a smaller level. When a leader fails, the same deed results in exponential disaster. Leaders have a few added pressures that make sexual temptation even more of a potential liability. That's why those who desire to keep their sexuality in a healthy state need clear spiritual power and direction.

Why do so many spiritual leaders seem to struggle in this area?

Leaders often have strong libidos. You may not find hard research stating this case, but a modest look at the lives of leaders, certain non-scientific writings on achievement, and the grapevine show that most leaders seem to have consistently strong sexual energy. Maybe it's a part of "achiever" wiring. But a "risk-taking, pushing-the-envelope, never-satisfied-with-status-quo" attitude is common among leaders. That same driving spirit often finds itself in the bedroom and in other relationships.

Leaders experience significant stress. Leading is often filled with pressure created by being in the limelight, by the multitude of activities, by the people issues, and because organizational health relies on the leader's decisions. Even when an organization succeeds, the weight of continuing success can be overwhelming. When an organization is failing, the stress can be inversely burdensome. The day-in, day-out tension that leaders feel can make sexual activity a therapeutic release.

A common weakness that may lead to sexual temptation is the "fear of success" syndrome. Just when a leader sees significant progress or is about to emerge strongly, he or she may take the road of releasing this energy in unhealthy means as in an affair or other unacceptable behavior. The leader may want to be caught, wishing to fail, so that he or she no longer has to endure the pressures of succeeding. The illogical thinking goes like this: "I'm not going to step down or surrender, because that would appear weak and I would have to explain it to everyone. Therefore, I will do something immoral and socially unacceptable where I will be forced to resign." The result, quite often, is that the leader is caught, resigns, and thus escapes the success that he or she feels undeserving of or loathes due to the stress.

The social pressure to perform based on the perceptions and predictions of others can be significant. We see this almost daily in the unhealthy courses that many celebrities choose.

Leaders are often given a romantic aura of sexual energy by followers. Natural leaders often possess personal charisma. This charm has a way of getting people's attention and wooing them over to a certain cause or idea. Charisma isn't bad in and of itself; its power of attraction gets people to listen to you, and that's a very important part of leading.

Whether it's sex appeal, charm, or just a sense of presence, leaders often use it for their benefit in leading. Because leadership is a relational process, people skills of all sorts can be tools for leading. Leaders draw more attention than others because of their exposure. People see and hear leaders in the limelight and feel as though they know them. They create one-way relationships with leaders, even if they don't know them. These relationships can turn into feelings of friendship and even romance. While the leader looks at a follower as merely a team member, the follower may load the relationship with sexual overtones. Any private attention that the leader gives the follower can ignite this energy.

Another way leaders influence others is by the sheer power they exude by their position of authority or their personal influence. People often want to share the feeling of power that a leader holds. One way to do this is to engage the leader through a sexual weakness.

The addictive power of leadership can cause them to flaunt their influence over others. Power can be an aphrodisiac. It is also addictive. People who hold power can be attractive to others, simply because they possess power. Naïve leaders assume that they possess some sexual attraction because of who they are rather than because of the leadership role itself. The same person outside of a leader role might have far less sex appeal. Undisciplined people can be tempted to abuse this power and attraction to manipulate people and use them for their own sexual pleasures. Spiritual leaders must be aware that these real possibilities exist in their role as leaders. When a leader consciously or unconsciously picks up flirtation signals from others, he or she may feed off this attention.

There can be a very fine line between the engaging aura of a charismatic leader and sexually laced flirtation. The problem is even more complicated because one person may be virtually innocuous in his or her motives, but the other person perceives something more in the relationship. While they may not consummate the sexual act with everyone they sense this energy with, leaders may feel the capacity and invitation to further such relations more often than non-leaders do. When leaders use their power to catalyze relationships that have unhealthy sexual content to them, they cross the line to using leadership for their own personal gratification.

Q HOW CAN SPIRITUAL LEADERS AVOID MISUSING SEXUAL ENERGY?

*Guard the good deposit that was entrusted to you —
guard it with the help of the Holy Spirit who lives in us.
(2 Timothy 1:14)*

In this verse, the word "guard" has the same root as "prophylactic," literally "to preserve," "to stand between." Here are some spiritual prophylactics that help guard your soul from the temptation of inappropriate expressions of sexuality. While the following protective strategies can work for everyone, they're vital for leaders.

Mend your fences. Relationships require various kinds of emotional fences, hedges, and boundaries if they are to stay healthy. Sometimes sexual boundaries include physical ones as well. Even innocent leaders can get caught in compromising situations when they fail to guard their boundaries.

Boundaries include the amount of time you spend with team members with whom you sense a possible attraction or who may be attracted to you. Modern work and ministry situations put people into potentially compromising situations, often more than in previous times. For example, e-mail connections can foster emotional attachments too easily, conveniently, and discreetly. So, establish formal protocol regarding private communications, meetings, travel, and counseling. Far too many innocent people have been caught up in friendships turned sexual because they spent inordinate amounts of time together.

[Potiphar] left in Joseph's care everything he had; with Joseph in charge, he did not concern himself with anything except the food he ate. Now Joseph was well-built and handsome, and after a while his master's wife took notice of Joseph and said, "Come to bed with me!"

But he refused. "With me in charge," he told her, "my master does not concern himself with anything in the house; everything he owns he has entrusted to my care. No one is greater in this house than I am. My master has withheld nothing from me except you, because you are his wife. How then could I do such a wicked thing and sin against God?" And though she spoke to Joseph day after day, he refused to go to bed with her or even be with her.

One day he went into the house to attend to his duties, and none of the household servants was inside. She caught him by his cloak and said, "Come to bed with me!" But he left his cloak in her hand and ran out of the house. . . .

When his master heard the story his wife told him, saying, "This is how your slave treated me," he burned with anger. Joseph's master took him and put him in prison, the place where the king's prisoners were confined. But while Joseph was there in the prison, the LORD was with him; he showed him kindness and granted him favor in the eyes of the prison warden. (Genesis 39:6-12,19-21)

A perception of indiscretion often has the same effect as a real one. While others' perceptions may not be accurate, they often result in loss of leadership because, in leading, perceptions are reality. In the verses above, if Joseph is guilty of anything, it's of being in a place where he could even be accused of an indiscretion.

Another boundary is being cautious in hiring situations. Try to get input from others regarding new team members. When a leader has the power to hire staff, it can become a hidden motive to surround himself or herself with temptations. Does this mean you only hire people you have an aversion to? Not necessarily. But if you're hiring people based on their skills and experience *and* due to their sex appeal, you run the risk of using your power to create a potentially sexual situation. Prayer and consultation can provide key input with such borderline situations. If your work allows it, securing a spousal "okay" is another hiring boundary.

Keep leisure and social times at a level of casual professionalism. Guard against phone and e-mail communication that is overtly personal or potentially suggestive. Establishing guarded emotions is akin to a force field that fends off enemy attacks in a science fiction story.

Create accountability with people who have permission to confront you. Perhaps the single most important spiritual-growth element a leader can establish is loving accountability. Because leaders are in the precarious situation of being busy and influential, establishing proper accountability is challenging.

When Nathan confronted King David after his tryst with Bathsheba, he made up a story to get David to admit his own failure, perhaps because Nathan was too nervous to confront David directly (2 Samuel 12). People in leadership run the risk of intimidating and punishing those who confront them. Add to this the human dilemma of pride, and you create an environment where leaders work in accountability vacuums, often resulting in their own demise.

If possible, find someone who knows you well but is not in a role where they will be rewarded or punished for raising honest accountability issues. The best form of this is a two-way accountability relationship, where both parties hold each other accountable. If one person is the subject of another's questioning, it can build up resentment in the person who is being held accountable. Establishing mutually acceptable game rules and then testing them over time in consistent meetings are the best ways to develop trust among peers.

Trust and confidence are vital to personal accountability. If leaders sense that their open sharing will make the light of day and be used against them, they'll likely avoid any confessions and reject true accountability.

Admit your vulnerability. Thinking "it will never happen to me" is a sign that you are naïve (not a position of strength) or overly confident (a position of weakness). The man in the Bible who is the only one given the description of "knowing the heart of God" is a guy who slept with another man's wife (King David). Unless you've got a better God-given description on your résumé and have had more of your praise choruses published in Scripture than this man, you're at least as vulnerable as he was. To pretend that temptation doesn't exist or to criticize others for their moral failures is to communicate a blind spot. The slogan "There but for the grace of God go I" is a humble reality check for all of us who are prone to elevate our level of spiritual prowess and moral mettle. Humility denotes a porous soul that is able to retain the power of the Holy Spirit. A haughty attitude reflects a "Scotchgarded" heart, where the Spirit rolls off without being absorbed. Such a soul is ripe for a fall.

Years ago, during the falls of several televangelists, I was in a small discipleship group led by author and pastor Ray Ortlund. One morning at the start of our meeting, a few of us were tossing our barbs at the fallen Christian celebrities. Ray hadn't said a word, even though he was a respected leader among religious broadcasters. After awhile, he quietly commented, "You know, we're all just one act away from these brothers." The conversation ended. Everyone was quiet, and we all dropped our verbal rocks.

How Can Spiritual Leaders Avoid Other Temptations of Leadership?

The most critical tactic for avoiding becoming a statistic is to pay attention to the vital signs of your spirituality. When you're not renewing yourself and observing the signs of spiritual growth, you're heading for a disaster—whether it's a crash or a slow fade into oblivion.

A similar but more realistic metaphor for leading is this: Imagine driving a pickup truck with dual fuel tanks, a primary and a reserve. The secondary one is much smaller, designed for a short stint before refueling. When the larger one goes dry, the vehicle automatically switches to the reserve.

This is similar to what happens when a spiritual leader runs low spiritually. The inner switch from the primary spiritual power to the human ability reserve is often invisible to the outside observer. Sometimes the leader doesn't even know what's happened because he or she is focused on driving the organization forward. The demands and expectations are present, regardless of the leader's spiritual condition. So, out of necessity and with a natural desire to lead, the leader performs leadership duties out of sheer human ability, devoid of significant spiritual power. The results of leading under human power and wisdom are far less desirable than those of leading under God's power.

This person is busy. Things appear to be getting done, so no one suggests that anything is amiss. But at this point, the spiritual leader has ceased to be a spiritual leader and has transitioned to being just a leader. A non-discerning leader will continue in this mode indefinitely, regardless of the viable signs that he or she is no longer leading from a spiritual power source. If he or she doesn't change course and make corrections, this leader will soon end up on the spiritual wreckage heap, in spite of impressive wins managed by human skill and gifting.

Because spiritual stamina ebbs and flows with the demands put upon it, spiritual leaders must realize their limitations. Jesus knew when it was time to say good night to the masses, push the "staff" into a boat, close up shop, and head to the hills to be alone with his Father. The demands were endless. The stack of "While You Were Out" message slips from the sick, possessed, lost, hungry, blind, and lame was huge, but Jesus set them to the side of his desk in order to recharge his spiritual batteries.

Most leaders err more than they think in the area of spiritual refueling. Their energy tanks switch to reserve far more than they realize. Because life and ministry move so fast, we hardly notice when we transition from spiritual leading to human leading.

Obviously, just because you have energy in your spiritual tank doesn't mean you're using it. You can manually override the system and rely on the spare tank. But when the spiritual tank is empty, no amount of manual override or earnest trying can manufacture genuine spiritual energy. Synthetic fuels are a dime a dozen, but nothing has been found to come close to replacing the stamina, wisdom, and effectiveness of authentic leading from a spiritual power source. Therefore, we need to discern signs of when our soul is growling for nutritional food.

What are the stall warnings for spiritual leaders about to fall? How does a spiritual leader know when his or her soul needs refueling? What are the signs or sounds of running on the reserve tank? The symptoms aren't always obvious. If they were, far fewer spiritual leaders would suffer burnout and failure. If leaders don't learn to discern these warning signs, they'll undoubtedly become victims of a crash-refuel cycle. That's the path many of us take. We don't realize that we're low on fuel until we crash-land a few meetings, relationships, or tasks. When we see our dilemma, we pull back a bit, regroup, focus on God, and take off again. But with every crash comes baggage, messes to clean up, and problems to fix. Some crashes are terminal; we or those around us never recover. This up-and-down roller coaster is inefficient and unnecessary.

Want to fail spiritually? You can find these clues to when leading becomes more human-fueled than Spirit-powered:

1. Relationships begin to fray or grow cool. Because spiritual fruit is most evident in attitudes toward others, a lack of fruit usually appears first via interpersonal interactions. In order to avoid interactions, we often distance ourselves from others or others from us.

2. Irritability and impatience over minor issues increase. When sparks fly and satirical words emerge over everyday minutia, the friction often reveals a lack of spiritual lubricant.

3. Ebb in joy and peace in leading: While leading is not always "fun," it should provide a consistent degree of fulfillment and satisfaction. When we begin to loathe leading, we may not have lost our calling as much as our Caller.

4. No or few active accountability systems in place: Everyone needs a word of encouragement or kick in the pants from time to time. If you can't put your finger on a recent and honest accountability contact, consider yourself at risk.

5. A schedule reflecting little time invested in prayer and worship: Calendar and checkbook are the two best priority revealers. Would there be sufficient evidence to convict you of being spiritual, if prayer and worship were crimes?

HOW MUCH CHRISTIAN COMMUNITY SHOULD BE ON A SPIRITUAL LEADER'S SCHEDULE?

Besides personal accountability, one of the best ways spiritual leaders can make sure they refuel their spiritual tank is to make sure that they're actively involved in Christian community. This can be tough for some leaders to assess because they may be leading the very spiritual community that can boost their spiritual power.

So if you can't "feel" or "sense" the big "E" on your spiritual fuel tank, just assume the needle is closing in on empty if you can't count at least three or four corporate worship services, Bible studies, or spiritual small-group connections in the last month. Spiritual fuel typically has a short shelf life. Our spiritual batteries only keep a charge for so long. We need to recharge them whether they're used or not.

> *When the dew was gone, thin flakes like frost on the ground appeared on the desert floor. When the Israelites saw [the manna], they said to each other, "What is it?" For they did not know what it was.*
>
> *Moses said to them, "It is the bread the LORD has given you to eat. This is what the LORD has commanded: 'Each one is to gather as much as he needs. Take an omer for each person you have in your tent.' "*
>
> *The Israelites did as they were told; some gathered much, some little. And when they measured it by the omer, he who gathered much did not have too much, and he who gathered little did not have too little. Each one gathered as much as he needed.*
>
> *Then Moses said to them, "No one is to keep any of it until morning." However, some of them paid no attention to Moses; they kept part of it until morning, but it was full of maggots and began to smell. So Moses was angry with them. Each morning everyone gathered as much as he needed, and when the sun grew hot, it melted away. (Exodus 16:14-21)*

God took care of his people in the desert by providing a bread-like substance called manna. The interesting thing about manna is that it was temporary. If you tried to hoard it, it would rot. While storing heaps of spiritual food is tempting at times and can make us think we are becoming incredibly strong, what goes unused is wasted. We must go out regularly to gather our spiritual food.

While Lone Ranger Christians exist, those who grow solely from personal Bible study, religious TV programming, and Internet soul-grow websites are very rare. It's practically impossible to stay spiritually online with God outside of live Christian community. While three or four times a month is a minimum, it's even better to shoot for weekly congregational worship and at least a couple times a month of small-group community. If extra work hours, travel, family time, or the business meetings at the golf course have put a squeeze play on corporate worship commitment, you can safely assume that your spiritual gas tank is on low or—quite frankly—sucking fumes.

Over my years in ministry, I've seen this as a general but true rule of thumb. Obviously, you can show up for church and not get your tank filled. It's akin to driving through a gas station without stopping at the pump. I've seen people in church who run on adrenaline so much during the week that when they stop to listen, they fall asleep. I haven't seen many God-by-osmosis techniques, although some believe in the power of subliminal suggestion.

Other achiever types I know attend church but can't get their minds off of business. Sermon illustrations intended to feed their souls instead further their work. While you can show up for Bible study and worship and not recharge, I've rarely seen spiritually hot people who were not in regular large- and small-group worship and Bible study.

How Much Personal Time with God Should Be on a Spiritual Leader's Schedule?

This is another vital test for determining the fuel level of your spiritual energy and dependence on God. Those of us who think just going to church or attending a weekly Bible study is sufficient for maintaining our spiritual intake are sadly mistaken. Maybe this simple thought is a light-bulb insight into why you don't have a closer walk with God. Even those of us raised in the churchgoing habit tend to underestimate the spiritual power that comes only from prolonged personal time with God. When we heavily rely on formal gatherings for our spiritual nurturing, we tend to be spiritual when the conditions of that environment are present. But when we leave these conditions and return to the environment of the office, home, and friendships, we face a good likelihood of returning to our original condition. Psychologists refer to this as conditioning. Take away the stimuli and you lose the response.

What needs to change is your "invironment," your inner conditions. This happens primarily as you nurture your private time with God. Cell phones, e-mail, and electronic living are all great for work and home, but lousy for spiritual growth. You can't "nuke" a relationship with God.

We need to consider that the farming metaphors used in the Bible may not simply be a result of the era in which they were taught. They're ageless. Farmers have yet to develop instant livestock or overnight crops. Just as marriages or any other significant relationships require both quality and quantity time if intimacy and depth are to occur, your relationship with God needs those qualities as well. One-minute devotionals can be great snack foods. But spiritual junk food, while getting you by, will never empower you for the workload of leading.

One way of assessing spiritual capacity is to look at the time you've spent alone with God in the last week or two. The old verbiage is "quiet time," but that may or may not be a realistic option. Sometimes we need noisy time with God just to keep our short attention spans tracking. Higher-octane people often experience quiet time that becomes a racket due to the noise in their heads. Leaders tend to be faster trackers for the most part, higher-energy people who are constantly pondering, thinking, strategizing, taking in and processing information. The pursuit of consistent, quality quiet time can be a route to guilt, frustration, and defeat.

God will take any time you give him—quiet, noisy, or other. The point is that you must spend adequate time with the true CEO, Divine Consultant, and Master Mind if you want to operate and succeed as a spiritual leader. Bible study resources, worship music, and spiritual-living books can provide structure for this; most of us do poorly without some structure and direction.

Centuries of God seekers and finders have yet to discover a substitute for adequate time alone with God. Schedule appointments with God as you would with your client, stockholder, friend, child, or spouse. If you can't find at least three or four periods of twenty to thirty minutes each week, chances are high that you're running near empty spiritually. And this time isn't always exciting—refueling your soul can be as exciting as gassing up your car. It might even feel like a chore. But the discipline of doing it will keep you focused on God.

I remember riding on the playground merry-go-round. We played a game where everyone would jump on and one of the strongest, fastest children would grab the bars and run alongside the merry-go-round. Faster, faster he ran. Those of us onboard clung to the bars, hugging the floor so as not to spin off. When the speed became fast enough, one by one, kids would fly off into the sand as their strength gave out. The last one remaining won.

The sheer speed of life, combined with our human nature, pulls us away from being centered on God. We have to cling, grab, and muster our strength to keep our souls from flinging off into the realm of human power and motivations. As soon as we let down our guard and lose our intentionality, we doom our leadership to human instead of spiritual centeredness.

"Watch and pray so that you will not fall into temptation. The spirit is willing, but the body is weak." (Matthew 26:41)

A Spiritual Leader's Outward Life

Why is attitude so vital in the role of a spiritual leader?

Why is power potentially toxic to spiritual leading?

How are talent and gifting adversarial to spiritual leading?

*How do position and success make us vulnerable
as spiritual leaders?*

How does the stress of leading weaken willpower?

How does soul nurturing change a leader's perspective?

How does the tyranny of the urgent make us vulnerable?

If leaders are to be servants, why do they often get paid more?

WHY IS ATTITUDE SO VITAL IN THE ROLE OF A SPIRITUAL LEADER?

Do you know the number-one complaint among employees? "It's too cold."

Now guess the second most common gripe: "It's too hot."

If the temperature of our workplace were the extent of our leadership problems, we'd be happy campers! But this little factoid is a good metaphor for understanding the role of a leader's attitude. When you enter your house or office and the temperature feels too hot or too cold, you go to the thermostat and adjust it. In a way, the leader's attitude sets the thermostat for an organization. Most often, if you're upbeat and excited as the leader, people will respond similarly. If you're a downer—negative and cranky—expect the same from your team members. The responsibility for establishing the climate control is primarily upon the leader. The word "responsibility" means literally, "the ability to respond." If you don't monitor your own attitude, your organization will behave in a Jekyll and Hyde manner, hot and cold, up and down.

Remember when you were a child, how much Mom or Dad's bad mood affected a car ride? Mom and Dad have great influence over the atmosphere of a family. The same is true of a leader in an organization, often in ways that most leaders don't realize. The reason is that influence serves as a magnifying glass. Just as the sun's light through a magnifying glass can burn leaves, so the attitude of the leader is more intensely felt than that of others. Because of this multiplication effect, leaders must be strategic about cultivating their attitudes. They're reckless if they live by feelings or if they allow their emotions to haphazardly affect others within an organization. Insensitive leaders don't care about the fallout of what they say or the actions they take.

Another reason a leader's attitude is so vital is that a majority of followers have an external locus of control. That's a fancy phrase meaning that people allow events and circumstances outside of themselves to control their perceptions and emotions. "It's a crummy day; looks like rain." "Oh no, the stock market dropped another fifty points." "I can't believe what that guy in traffic did to me." Listen to casual conversations and you'll hear people reveal their external orientation.

On the other hand, leaders need to be people who operate primarily from an internal locus of control. That's why spiritual leading becomes an important part of organizational effectiveness, because the internal world is where leaders secure their ability to determine their attitudes and responses to external events. Leading is primarily an inner game, requiring us to respond to circumstances, but not from an external orientation.

In baseball, a coach gives signals to the players, telling them to bunt, steal, hit and run, or hold up. The participants exchange few words, but communication is taking place on the field. Organizations and team members look to leaders for their cues. Followers want game signs to help them know how they should behave in a situation.

This rule of communication holds truer within leadership than in general: You cannot *not* communicate. What you say and don't say, how you say it, the look on your face, the intonation of your voice, and the tiny glimmers in your eye can convey hope, despair, disapproval, acceptance, anger, dishonesty, or any number of nonverbal messages. If a leader sends mixed signals, confusion prevails. When a leader says something positive but his or her prevailing attitude is one of fear and gloom, most people will respond to the latter.

"It's not fair! That's too much pressure for any leader." Welcome to the club. Fair or not, it's a reality in leadership. Thus, the responsibility of leaders to cultivate their own attitudes becomes an important part of their role. Ask the questions, *Do I want all of my followers and collaborators to respond as I am? What would happen if everyone's attitude was like mine right now?* The more influential the leader, the greater the impact upon leadership. A gallon of boiling water thrown into the ocean won't change the temperature. The same gallon added to a quart of water will significantly change it.

In Numbers 13–14, when the ten spies brought back negative reports, Moses, Joshua, and Caleb maintained a "can do" attitude. Unfortunately, their influence was too small to significantly raise the temperature of the masses, and they failed to go forward. The human propensity to believe negative reports faster than positive ones is probably a symptom of our spiritual depravity. Our culture often makes hope the underdog.

Marketers know that customers will repeatedly tell friends about a bad experience at a store far more than they'll talk about a positive one. Gossip travels at the speed of sound. Bad news gets attention: just look at the dominant content of news programs and magazines. This makes the job of the leader more difficult, because our battle of purveying hope is an uphill challenge.

WHY IS POWER POTENTIALLY TOXIC TO SPIRITUAL LEADING?

Certain phrases become well worn because of their basic truth. One such phrase is, "Power corrupts and absolute power corrupts absolutely." Leadership that is powerless is not leadership. It's a hollow position at best. Impotent figureheads and hole fillers are plentiful.

The very nature of leading requires power and influence. Unfortunately, the desire to be in control responds to the inherent nature of power. The first recorded temptation was about control: If you eat of the fruit, you'll become like God (Genesis 3:1-5). We're tempted by the feeling of being important, being able to change circumstances, and appearing to be a go-to person to help people with their problems. Power isn't bad. Jesus couldn't have healed without power, drawn crowds without it, or performed miracles without it. But power is often like a bull's-eye for temptation. Satan tried to get Jesus to flaunt his power in his wilderness temptation (Matthew 4). Countless leaders fall prey to the alluring seduction of power.

The essence of sin revolves around the issue of power . . . who's in control. Every fruit of sin (lying, stealing, adultery, cheating, envy, jealousy, greed, and so on) actually stems from the root of power—when we try to call the shots instead of letting God. So when leaders who are human are put in charge of organizations, resources, and people, it's akin to putting the proverbial fox in charge of the chicken coop. By nature, we're prone to want to run things ourselves. When other people begin to expect us to take charge and to usurp power to get groups of people to stay on task, they're aiding and abetting our spiritual dysfunction. Being in charge as a leader is a natural thing for many of us, but to turn that power over to God and rely on him is somewhat of an unnatural act. We want to take the ball and run with it, not pass it off to God. We then rely on human strength and stamina instead of spiritual.

So what's the solution? The word "solution" here does not suggest that a simple problem/solution relationship exists. The antidotes to any of the spiritual hazards of leading discussed in this section are difficult. They all have to do with character qualities, few of which come easily. In this case, the way to counteract pride is to nurture humility.

One of the ways God cultivates humility in leaders is by taking them through times of testing. He doesn't necessarily create the trials, but his goal is that through times of brokenness, leaders will expand their capacity for him and become pliable and responsive to him. This process can come via a variety of sources: failure, moral lapse, ill health, financial loss, relational collapse, or emotional burnout. Any of these events are means that God uses to develop humility.

The word "humility" comes from the same root as the word "humus," which is the rich, fertile soil that contains decaying matter. When the old nature dies in us, it yields a healthy combination with God's Spirit. Humility is to the soul what fertilizer is to a garden.

Submitting to God's power and his control requires a disciplined and resolute person. Leaders must learn this as an intentional practice, much like hurdle runners practice both running and jumping without losing their stride. The task is doubly difficult for leaders. When we feel like we must make the decisions, call the shots, and power up via our God-given talents without God-present power, we're apt to lead poorly.

Truly submitting to God involves consciously pursuing his will through prayer, servanthood, and seeking him. When we let God be in control and we run the ship as second in command as opposed to first, we benefit our own souls as well as the souls of those we lead.

HOW ARE TALENT AND GIFTING ADVERSARIAL TO SPIRITUAL LEADING?

Many leaders have abilities that are necessary to manage complex situations. They also have supplemental gifts such as communication skills, people smarts, and organizational and/or problem-solving abilities. Most of these gifts are God-given, and they're necessary to win the respect of followers. Unfortunately, the same gifts also tempt leaders to rely on their own abilities instead of God.

> *Jesus looked at him and said, "How hard it is for the rich to enter the kingdom of God! Indeed, it is easier for a camel to go through the eye of a needle than for a rich man to enter the kingdom of God." (Luke 18:24-25)*

Even though Jesus was specifically referring to financial wealth in this context, the same concept applies to any sort of wealth—talent, abilities, network, and gifts. The point is that "wealthy" people have the tendency to rely on themselves instead of God. Jesus wasn't, as some people have concluded, anti-money. Rather, he knew how easy it is to rely on your own strengths. Most of us don't have to pray "give us this day, our daily bread," because we know where today's and tomorrow's bread are coming from. Not depending on God hamstrings all "wealthy" people with strong human resources, including most leaders.

How do leaders learn to rely on God?

Let go. Oddly, this may be the hardest thing of all, because people who are used to being in control have trouble giving God control. God has given leaders a set of power tools: gifts, talents, intelligence, social and organizational smarts. But our natural tendency is to use them under our own power. Failing to let God use our abilities, we fight to make things happen under our own energy. While these gifts may take us far, they're apt to yield stressful and marginal results.

I once heard the true story of a man who was paddling a canoe down a river. When he came to a dam, he ignored the warning signs as well as the shouts of fellow boaters who had rowed to the side and taken their boats out of the water. Incapacitated by alcohol, the inebriated man somehow thought he could manage the flow over the large dam. Ignoring the calls of others, which were now drowned out by the sounds of crashing water, the man took his canoe over the dam. He plunged into the frigid water below, bobbing up in the white, foamy maelstrom. He went under and came up again. The onlookers high above the river below were powerless to reach the man. He came up again, gasping for air and fighting with all his might to swim to the side. But the currents were too wild and strong. After a minute or two, the man lost the battle and was pulled under. Moments later, his limp, lifeless body came bursting to the top, a few feet downstream. The current that pulled him under had released him into the calm waters past the falls.

The power of the current did what the man was unable to do himself. If he'd quit trying to save himself and let the current take him, it would have safely delivered him into the tranquil waters. But his natural tendency to fight the flow became his ruin.

Revel in weakness. When we rely on our strengths as our primary mode of operation, we can easily supplant God. If we have a bum leg, we rest on a crutch. Although using the crutch can become second nature, it's never as natural as our leg. Relying on God as our source of strength and direction can become familiar, but it must begin intentionally. Our natural inclination is to revert back to our bum leg.

> *That is why, for Christ's sake, I delight in weaknesses, in insults, in hardships, in persecutions, in difficulties. For when I am weak, then I am strong.* (2 Corinthians 12:10)

In this verse, Paul is saying that when we rely on our greatest strength, it's still the equivalent to a bum leg compared to God's supernatural abilities. Consider your strengths as weaknesses and treat them in such a way that you humbly rely on God. The greatest weakness empowered by God is greater than the best human-generated strength.

Remember that God owns your gifts. The biblical concept of stewardship teaches us that we're not the owners of our abilities; we're simply stewards of them. The spiritual leader understands that he or she is little more than a manager of God-given resources.

> *"Again, [the kingdom of heaven] will be like a man going on a journey, who called his servants and entrusted his property to them. To one he gave five talents of money, to another two talents, and to another one talent, each according to his ability. Then he went on his journey." (Matthew 25:14-15)*

This Scripture, a part of what is known as the Parable of the Talents, is interesting because the employees were given money "according to their abilities." Thus, talents are not so much representative of gifts as they are of opportunities. The opportunity to influence and lead is a very noble role; but for the spiritual leader, it's a God-given opportunity created by God-given abilities.

Jesus told another story about the human tendency to take ownership of our gifts:

"Listen to another parable: There was a landowner who planted a vineyard. He put a wall around it, dug a winepress in it and built a watchtower. Then he rented the vineyard to some farmers and went away on a journey. When the harvest time approached, he sent his servants to the tenants to collect his fruit.

"The tenants seized his servants; they beat one, killed another, and stoned a third. Then he sent other servants to them, more than the first time, and the tenants treated them the same way. Last of all, he sent his son to them. 'They will respect my son,' he said.

"But when the tenants saw the son, they said to each other, 'This is the heir. Come, let's kill him and take his inheritance.' So they took him and threw him out of the vineyard and killed him." (Matthew 21:33-39)

Who could blame the renters? After all, they were the ones who had tilled the soil, sweat in labor, and risked the harvest. But none of this changed the fact that they were renters, not owners. Leaders tend to be gifted, confident, take-charge people who are tempted to push God out the door, resulting in non-spiritual leadership. Spiritual leaders realize that they are renters and managers, not owners, of their gifts and abilities.

How Do Position and Success Make Us Vulnerable as Spiritual Leaders?

Many people don't understand the psychological stress that success and fame create for people who are in the limelight. Generally, the more success, the more difficult it is to maintain a humble, God-dependent attitude. When people look to you for solutions, applaud your expertise, and call you up for favors, the thrill can create self-deception. The very fact that so many people look to you for wisdom, decisions, advice, and even permission can create an illegitimate sense of self-importance. You begin to believe your own press releases.

Leadership roles often provide people with opportunities to experience more success than others. The highest-paid workers in the United States are CEOs and top executives. The gap is widening between what top executives and common employees make. When stock prices and profit margins soar, stockholders, media, well-wishers, and wannabes bow to the god-like qualities of the leader.

The seduction of success is very strong. While we start to believe followers who applaud our achievements, at the same time we insulate ourselves from critics and those who would hold us accountable. The greater the success, the less we see the need for God. Unlike the common person, leaders have unique opportunities to experience the thrills of fruitfulness and applause. We justify these perks by pointing out our risks, hard work, courage in the face of criticism, and tenacious efforts. "I deserve my rewards. I'm the one who paid the price as the leader." Being in the limelight and performing the duties of a spokesperson can feed unhealthy ego desires and pride, which are antithetical to spirituality.

How can leaders avoid the success syndrome? They must learn to work in spiritually toxic environments. Just as medical people wear masks and rubber gloves around body fluids, and nuclear engineers take necessary precautions when dealing with hazardous wastes, leaders need protective measures to shield themselves from potentially toxic thoughts and emotions. Retaining loving accountability is one of the best preservatives of spiritual character.

Who knows you for who you are outside of the head office, minus the titles, or knew you when you were merely latent potential? For some it's a spouse, or a friend who has known you in childhood, or a trusted confidant. Leaders who avoid being accountable to such people tend to succumb to pride, the archenemy of spirituality. The spiritual disciplines of solitude and anonymous giving are healthy barriers that help restrain us from such arrogance. When the limelight creates a desire for more of the same, going away to a lonely place or serving and donating where no one knows can be a positive adjustment.

Savvy leaders understand how weak they are when left to their own devices. They never underestimate their ability to be deceived by the seductive powers of position and pride. They intentionally build in warning systems—generally friends—who can lovingly let them know when pride appears to be a potential problem. These people aren't subordinates, collaborators, or followers—they're separate from the control issues of the leader. History is full of honest but loyal followers who told the truth only to be blacklisted, relegated to a dead-end position, fired, or even executed. Nonspiritual leaders create artificial environments where they can live out their fantasies of perfection and effectiveness. The reason emperors can walk down the street without their clothes is because they have eliminated neutral, loving feedback.

Spiritual leaders know that the criticism of a supporter is more valuable than flattery of an opponent: "Wounds from a friend can be trusted, but an enemy multiplies kisses" (Proverbs 27:6). Who is apt to tell you when you're "too big for your shoes"? If someone were to do this, what would your response be? Would you punish or alienate him or her?

HOW DOES THE STRESS OF LEADING WEAKEN WILLPOWER?

Stress is internal pressure created by external forces and internal responses. Leading isn't for the timid or weak, for it tends to be a high-pressure activity. That's why some people who've been in high-powered roles in the past avoid similar ones because they either burned out or no longer enjoy the stress of leading. Strong business leaders sometimes avoid leading roles in ministry because they are battle-worn from their work. On days off, many leaders are the antithesis of a leader because they feel weary from decision making. Reaching goals, managing change, creating innovation, and being responsible for the lives and souls of others have a way of wearing on even the strongest leaders. The best leaders can live very lonely lives as they bear the burden of an organization as no one else. That's the down side of leading.

When negative stress continues over a period of time, leaders can begin to cave in from the pressure. Those who haven't learned to resort to spiritual means and faith in God often pursue unhealthy stress reduction; this can be through materialism, an obsession with a hobby, extreme sports, sexual affairs, or substance abuse. These crutches are artificial resources used either to deaden the pain or to provide temporary escapes from the stress. One CEO said that he was invited to a leaders' group where the members did semi-annual getaways and where everyone invited his girlfriend instead of his wife. While "keeping a girl on the side" seems very natural for some, this and similar practices obviously weaken the moral fiber of a leader. Non-spiritual leaders find such vices justifiable because of the high stress their positions call them to endure.

Spiritual leaders can significantly reduce the stress they experience by understanding the difference between control and guidance. Leaders are guides, limited in what they can control. They realize that ultimate control is in God's hands. When our best efforts yield marginal results, we can't beat ourselves up or take it out on those around us (another popular leader strategy). Our job as spiritual leaders is to give both the failures and the successes to God. When we take on more than our fair share of control, we heap unrealistic expectations on ourselves and eventually buckle under the pressure. Leaders are often their own worst enemies because they overestimate what they're able to control through their own abilities.

Recognizing what is and isn't doable is a major issue in maturity and wisdom. Spiritual leaders seek wisdom that transcends their own capacities.

> *If any of you lacks wisdom, he should ask God, who gives generously to all without finding fault, and it will be given to him. (James 1:5)*

The Serenity Prayer is a powerful tool for leaders who want to take a spiritual approach to their calling: "God, grant me the serenity to accept the things I cannot change, the courage to change the things I can, and the wisdom to know the difference."

HOW DOES SOUL NURTURING CHANGE A LEADER'S PERSPECTIVE?

Perhaps the biggest single benefit of nurturing your soul as a leader is that it gives you perspective you can't get any other way. Because the soul of a person is equivalent to the hub of a wheel, staying centered is a very important element of balance. Leadership tends to magnify our strengths and weaknesses, so a leader with a soul off center wobbles more noticeably than anyone else. Spiritual leaders bear the burden of keeping themselves in balance so that their perspectives are truth-oriented.

For example, going through times of conflict with people creates negative stress. As is often said, "My job would be great, if it weren't for the people." Unfortunately, leaders can't adopt this philosophy, because their primary work is people—accomplishing what can only be achieved by people working together toward a common vision.

> *For I hear the slander of many; there is terror on every side; they conspire against me and plot to take my life.*

But I trust in you, O LORD; I say, "You are my God."
(Psalm 31:13-14)

Many are those who are my vigorous enemies; those
who hate me without reason are numerous. Those who
repay my good with evil slander me when I pursue
what is good. O LORD, do not forsake me; be not far
from me, O my God. Come quickly to help me, O Lord
my Savior. (Psalm 38:19-22)

Turning our relational struggles over to God is a primary
stress reducer for leaders. But how do leaders do that? Here
are a couple of ideas:

Staying centered must be a preoccupation for spiritual leaders.
When a leader is off-center, his or her perspective tends to
reflect human views that cause him or her to overestimate
negative or trivial issues. Spiritual leaders who stay centered
can discern the difference between minors and majors. When
we lose our perspective, minors become majors and majors
turn into minors. We argue and fret over issues that are petty
in terms of the big picture and long-term benefits.

"So do not worry, saying, 'What shall we eat?' or 'What
shall we drink?' or 'What shall we wear?' For the
pagans run after all these things, and your heavenly
Father knows that you need them. But seek first his
kingdom and his righteousness, and all these things will
be given to you as well. Therefore do not worry about
tomorrow, for tomorrow will worry about itself. Each
day has enough trouble of its own." (Matthew 6:31-34)

In the same way, the Spirit helps us in our weakness.
We do not know what we ought to pray for, but the
Spirit himself intercedes for us with groans that words
cannot express. And he who searches our hearts knows

the mind of the Spirit, because the Spirit intercedes for the saints in accordance with God's will. And we know that in all things God works for the good of those who love him, who have been called according to his purpose. (Romans 8:26-28)

Spiritual leading doesn't mean a stress-free existence. Leaders who claim to have no stress in their work are either overly disengaged and less effective or in a very temporary state of balance in their organizations. These balanced moments are necessary but rare in today's topsy-turvy times. Leading is stressful, period. Instead of whining and longing for a stress-free place, spiritual leaders need to employ natural and spiritual decompression techniques. Certainly exercise, developing positive friendships, nutritious eating, and sufficient sleep are as vital to leaders as to anyone else. But in addition to these, leaders can take advantage of spiritual means to handle their normal stress issues.

When anxiety was great within me, your consolation brought joy to my soul. (Psalm 94:19)

Humble yourselves, therefore, under God's mighty hand, that he may lift you up in due time. Cast all your anxiety on him because he cares for you. (1 Peter 5:6-7)

The psalms by Israel's King David are good examples of stress-reducing prayers. Some of them are far from holy sounding, but they are honest expressions of anger, loneliness, and stress that leaders experience. Instead of internalizing the pressure and playing games with God, David did a lot of dumping. God desires that of all of us, especially of those who lead. When leaders believe that God is somehow threatened or disconcerted when they honestly admit frustration, it means they have a misperception of our Creator. He's very concerned about the challenges we face as leaders, because he knows the potential impact we have—positive and negative—upon the people, organizations, and communities we serve. When we fail to turn our stress over to God, we're prime candidates for burnout as well as a disruption of fruitful service to others.

HOW DOES THE TYRANNY OF THE URGENT MAKE US VULNERABLE?

The demands of leading in changing organizations can require nearly supernatural energy. When you place an achiever type into an environment that seems to have endless needs, the chemistry is potentially toxic to the soul. When you add to that a sincere desire to serve people and help them, you commonly find leaders who are burning the candle at both ends.

Leaders are problem solvers and are drawn to oil squeaky wheels. The pressures of tasks and people can overly occupy any concerned person. Because leaders tend to have larger networks with more people answering to and needing responses from them, they can easily succumb to the pressure. Our addiction to adrenaline and movement keep us from investing in soul growth, which cannot be done satisfactorily on the run. Ultimately, the frenetic pace many of us leaders keep becomes our downfall.

Growing up on a farm in Iowa, I spent many days in the fields, fixing fences with my dad. Often we'd come to places in the fence where the ground below a post had eroded, leaving the post dangling in air, held up only by the wires. You can imagine the same thing when you think of a leader who has had a moral or emotional failure. At first, you wonder, "How did a person like that get into that position?" The person wasn't like that from the start. But gradually, the forces of stress and success eroded the foundation.

The sheer busyness of life in the fast lane preoccupies many leaders, so that maintaining their souls is no longer a priority. All the while, the demands are taking away inner ballast, creating a vacuum. Although the post appeared to be holding up the fencing, the post was actually being held up by the wires. Casual observation may make us think that the leader is holding up the organization, when actually it is supporting the leader.

The solution to the problem of consuming leadership opportunities may seem to be time management. Unfortunately, most time management concepts focus on better organization in order to glean more time. These are not unimportant, but the actual missing component is priority management.

Spirituality is about establishing the right priorities, those that will enhance our souls and nourish our relationship with our Creator. Because priorities are more what we do than what we say we value, priority management holds a greater benefit than time management. Leaders are forever performing triage, assigning importance and urgency to tasks at hand and allocating available resources. When a leader understands the importance of quiet time and soul growth, he or she will magically find time to invest in regular soul growth.

A wonderful model of balance and priority management was Jesus. We easily justify our busyness by suggesting that the pace of life in the early part of the twenty-first century is hectic. The organizational adage used to be *bigger is better*. Now *faster is better*. How can an ancient Jesus relate to the multi-tasking, super-stimulating pace of today's culture? You never see Jesus running around, telling people to take a number or frantically going both directions at the same time. But if you look beyond the surface, you realize that he was a man with a mission.

Jesus had a mere three years to establish his organization centered on a dozen untrained and questionably loyal staff. In mere months, he made more of a mark than any individual in history, yet we never see him rushing or hurried. Jesus didn't allow other people to pull his strings or move him from his intended course.

For example, at a wedding, the hosts ran out of wine early in the evening:

> *When the wine was gone, Jesus' mother said to him, "They have no more wine."*
>
> *"Dear woman, why do you involve me?" Jesus replied. "My time has not yet come." (John 2:3-4)*

While his response may sound disrespectful, Jesus knew that friends and relatives have a way of getting us off center.

At another time, we learn:

> *Very early in the morning, while it was still dark, Jesus got up, left the house and went off to a solitary place, where he prayed. Simon and his companions went to look for him, and when they found him, they exclaimed: "Everyone is looking for you!"*
>
> *Jesus replied, "Let us go somewhere else—to the nearby villages—so I can preach there also. That is why I have come." (Mark 1:35-38)*

Jesus' staff finds and informs him that he has several prospective followers waiting to see him. Jesus suggests they go do something else. What about public relations? What if these people are disappointed? What will they think? Jesus could make these priority decisions with confidence because he had spent time earlier in the day aligning himself with God. We often see Jesus getting away to center himself with God. After Jesus fed the five thousand,

> *Immediately [he] made the disciples get into the boat and go on ahead of him to the other side, while he dis-missed the crowd. After he had dismissed them, he went*

up on a mountainside by himself to pray. When evening
came, he was there alone. (Matthew 14:22-23)

Jesus apparently knew that the needs of people were endless.
If he was to make the greatest impact with his limited time
and presence, he had to take the time to nourish his soul.

A spiritual leader doesn't consider prayer, solitude, and
meditation as preparations for leading. He realizes that these
activities are actually a *part* of vibrant leading. Someone said,
"If I had to chop wood for eight hours, I'd sharpen my axe for
six." Perhaps that's an exaggeration, but wise mentors through
the years have expressed the importance of spending more
time with God when there is more to be accomplished.
Unfortunately, God rarely squeaks or squawks. He doesn't
leave us e-mails or phone messages.

If we don't take time with God, we leaders grab our oilcan
and run to the loudest squeak, not realizing that we're drasti-
cally low on oil. Sometimes we find ourselves going through
the motions of oiling people's squeaks, without noticing that
we've run out of oil long ago. For some followers, the mere
oiling behavior of a leader pacifies them temporarily, but the
squeaks tend to get louder than ever when the leader's oilcan
is empty. The Tin Man forgot to oil himself.

Not by coincidence, the Holy Spirit is symbolized by oil
throughout the Bible. Kings were anointed with oil in the Old
Testament as a sign of God's touch. Oil as a lubricant is a great
metaphor for keeping our internal machinery functioning.

My dad used to tell me that oil is the lifeblood of your car.
The fastest way to ruin an engine is to run it without oil. I
found that out the hard way. For a while in my twenties, John
Maxwell was kind enough to mentor me. One time, I was
driving him to a speaking engagement in southern California.
On our way back, the car started making funny noises. We
made it to a shop. The mechanics gave us some lame reason
for the behavior and sent us back on the road. Neither John

nor I was mechanically inclined. Not far down the highway, the car stopped again. When we got out, oil was leaking all over the ground. Obviously, we shouldn't have driven it after the first stop. We rented a car, and John had his car towed back to San Diego. I think I still have the recognition of being the only guy to ruin John Maxwell's car.

Soul squeaks show up in frayed relationships, sleepless nights, worry, anger, bad decisions, and burnout. Take time for frequent oil changes and be sure to add a quart here and there.

IF LEADERS ARE TO BE SERVANTS, WHY DO THEY OFTEN GET PAID MORE?

If you were to draw the flow chart or structure of an organization headed by a servant leader, what would it look like? One way would be to invert the pyramid, with the leader at the bottom—humble, serving God and others above himself or herself.

If that's the case, however, would a servant leader make less money? The issue of reward should be a matter of who brings the most benefit to the organization. If the servant leader is leading well, then his or her service is accomplishing more toward the goals of the organization than anyone else's. If this isn't the case, then the person shouldn't be rewarded most. A more difficult issue is proportion. Does the leader's pay and/or benefits reflect the difference between that person and other team members?

Can the organization afford to pay its leader what he or she deserves? Because high-quality leaders are in shortage and will probably remain so in the twenty-first century, chances are the sometimes high and seemingly inordinate salaries will continue.

The Bible speaks about paying people for what they agree to work for and treating employees fairly. It talks about rewarding those who produce. It speaks of not rewarding those who don't produce (Matthew 25). The biggest matter here is one of attitude. Servant leaders consider themselves to be servants, not better than others because they lead. Rewards, titles, positions, office size and location, and overall attention given the leader can certainly work against this attitude. Thus, combining a servant's heart and a leader's role can make for a difficult marriage.

The only way to accomplish servant leadership successfully is by spiritual means. Spiritual leaders resist thinking of themselves as leaders. They develop the self-image of a servant, first to their Creator and then to others. When you think about it, maintaining a servant self-image over the long haul is much easier than thinking of yourself as a leader. Servants have very few possessions. They have fewer expectations.

Grooming your image as a leader can require a huge amount of energy. You have to be careful of how others see you; you have to watch out for those vying for your position; and you have to be overly conscious of what others are thinking and saying. But because servants own and possess very little, they're able to put much more of their energy into their work and relationships. They are freer to lead. Although you can never be fully liberated from issues of image maintenance, you can certainly lessen them when you assume the attitude of a servant.

Spiritual leaders must buck the flow of society. In our culture, effective leaders are applauded. They're heralded with accolades, perks, benefits, and sizable paychecks. Followers have difficulty getting messages through to them or find it hard to meet them in person. Leaders eat in expensive boardrooms, have their own washrooms, and sit behind solid wood desks in offices with million-dollar views. Certainly, this doesn't reflect all leaders, but it does project an image of what leader wannabes strive to emulate.

Somehow this misses the point of what it means to be both spiritual and a leader. The wonderful thing, however, is that the spiritual servant leader has a better chance of making a splash. Why? Because so few leaders reflect this attitude, and yet so many followers hunger for this kind of leader.

A Spiritual Leader's Role

How does a spiritual leader prevent organizational stagnation?

How does a spiritual leader respond to the need for change?

How does a spiritual leader best use team members?

How do spiritual leaders develop new leaders?

How do spiritual leaders care for the spiritual side of their followers?

How do spiritual leaders create a culture that nurtures the soul?

What do relationships in an organization have to do with spiritual leadership?

What are some indicators of spiritual leading found in relationships and attitudes?

What happens when a spiritual leader fails?

What happens when the goal or the organization fails?

HOW DOES A SPIRITUAL LEADER PREVENT ORGANIZATIONAL STAGNATION?

There is a time for everything, and a season for every activity under heaven . . . [God] has made everything beautiful in its time. (Ecclesiastes 3:1,11)

Every living thing, organic or organizational, has a "time," a life cycle. There are beginnings, endings, and middle ages, short or long. Understanding this helps us better understand people, marriages, churches, businesses, and governments. Without intentional times of revival and innovation, living things will eventually peak, plateau, and decline. Food items in the back of your refrigerator eventually grow hair, and spiritual leaders can assume that mold is forming on their organization even before it's obvious.

The leadership part of spiritual leadership means that you are about changing, improving, and serving your organization by helping it become better. You're not just interested in maintaining. The spiritual part of spiritual leadership is about growth, bearing fruit, and maturity.

> *"No one sews a patch of unshrunk cloth on an old garment, for the patch will pull away from the garment, making the tear worse. Neither do men pour new wine into old wineskins. If they do, the skins will burst, the wine will run out and the wineskins will be ruined. No, they pour new wine into new wineskins, and both are preserved." (Matthew 9:16-17)*

> *"See, the former things have taken place, and new things I declare; before they spring into being I announce them to you." (Isaiah 42:9)*

> *"Forget the former things; do not dwell on the past. See, I am doing a new thing! Now it springs up; do you not perceive it? I am making a way in the desert and streams in the wasteland." (Isaiah 43:18-19)*

A theology of "new" helps us understand the spiritual side of change. God is always the same. He never changes (James 1:17; Hebrews 13:8). And one of the unchanging aspects of God is that he's always doing something new. For example, while the essence of worship never changes, the forms of worship are ever evolving so that they stay fresh, alive, and dynamic. Stale worship is an oxymoron. This is also true of organizations, whether they exist to provide service, technology, communication, education, or products. Maintenance is a sure sign of organizational death in the twenty-first century.

In addition to intellectual and statistical input, spiritual leaders rely heavily on their souls to discern the need for change. They implement faith by taking risks. Throughout history, people have stoned their prophets and scoffed at inventors and cutting-edge explorers. Why? By nature, most people are wired to resist newness. Their identities are heavily attached to keeping things the way they are. Their faith is more in the familiar than it is in the spirit of the new that God is doing. There will be friction, misunderstanding, and conflict.

By the time a majority of people have come to the conclusion that the old ways are used up, chances are that the organization has lost too much momentum and the window of opportunity may have closed. Only internally led leaders will have the guts to take the risks necessary to pursue change. Spiritual leaders are stewards responsible for using the organizational talents and resources to produce fruit, not lose it. Leaders willing to allow their organizations to stagnate are poor stewards who waste potential. Ultimately, they will be held accountable for burying their resources (Matthew 25).

How Does a Spiritual Leader Respond to the Need for Change?

Preventing stagnation is a proactive skill. It involves understanding the life cycle of a product, method, or organization. The goal is improvement, not merely rearranging the deck chairs on the *Titanic*. Many change agents equate being productive with keeping busy. Not all change is good. But denial runs strong in change-needy environments, where people avoid the need for change and buck the improvement.

The key is strategic change, which is where spiritual leadership is better than non-spiritual. The spiritual leader works from the inside out, not merely reacting to statistics and external factors. Hearing one's soul, discerning the best improvements, and sensing divine intervention are vital parts of twenty-first-century leading.

Another benefit of leading spiritually comes when implementing a plan for transition. An improvement plan is what you expect to become; it focuses on where you want to end up. But this is strategically different from a transition plan, which focuses on how your organization will get there, starting with where it is now in emotions, culture, felt-needs, communication, and relationships. Many plans for change fail because leaders misunderstand the difference between these two aspects: where to go and how to get there. You can know exactly where you want to go, but if you fail in getting there, it's wasted effort.

Spiritual leaders are better equipped to respond to the soft side of leading that transitioning is primarily about. Saying good-bye to old customs, feeling the fear and anger of people as they mourn their loss, and understanding the emotional side of change allows a spiritual leader to respond to these issues more effectively.

You can estimate how effectively a transition plan will work by looking at four factors: time, leader capacity, group readiness, time, and impact of change. By providing numerical estimates, you can plug in numbers and determine a Delta Factor, which can help you know what to expect from people. The formula looks like this:

$$\frac{(\text{Leader capacity} + \text{Group readiness}) \times \text{Time}}{\text{Impact of change}} = \text{Delta Factor}^2$$

Leader capacity: How capable is the leader? Strong leaders are able to pull off change quickly due to people skills, vision communication, organizational thinking, and personal influence. Estimate the level of leader capacity as follows:

> 1 for poor leader skills; 2 for modest leader skills; 3 for average leader skills; 4 for strong leader skills; 5 for excellent leader skills

Group readiness: How ready is your group or organization to accept this innovation and improvement? Do they feel and understand the problem? Most leaders fail by selling solutions instead of problems. But people don't want solutions for problems they can't see. Estimate readiness as follows:

> 1 for opposing the change; 2 for being happy where they are; 3 for being neutral to the change; 4 for feeling ready for the improvement; 5 for being excited about the improvement

Time: How fast do you plan to incorporate the improvement? Quicker change creates greater stress. Allowing more time often reduces tension. In a typical organization, here are the numerical figures that match the impact of time:

> 1 is for 0–6 months; 2 is for 6–12 months; 3 is for 1–2 years; 4 is for 2–3 years; 5 is for 3–5 years. At the speed of change in the twenty-first century, planning beyond five years is precarious at best. If time estimates are on the borders, round up or down appropriately.

Impact of change: How much will this improvement influence the organization? The bigger the impact, the slower you may want to pursue it. All change is not the same. Greater impact results in heightened stress.

1 for minimal impact that few will notice; 2 for noticeable but not large; 3 for noticeable, significant change, but not transformational; 4 for large change that all will notice and be affected by; 5 for transformational improvement that will change the very nature of the organization

Plug these numbers into the formula above. The result is the Delta Factor. With that numerical score, note the transition-effectiveness categories for your estimate:

0.4–1.5 — *Level 1:* Poor (fat chance; slim odds of surviving the change)

1.6–2.9 — *Level 2:* Fair (some bloodletting, loss, and struggle, but possible)

3.0–4.9 — *Level 3:* Positive (modest conflict, but nothing bad if you work it well)

5.0–20.9 — *Level 4:* Optimum (minor conflict, but with homework done, it's great)

21.0–50.0 — *Level 5:* Overly ripe (you're late, having lost good people and potential)

How Does a Spiritual Leader Best Use Team Members?

As a spiritual leader, you're in the people business. Your job is to build big people who in turn build strong organizations. Strong means more than size; it means high quality, health, and vitality. Spiritual leaders, far more than their non-spiritual counterparts, elevate the development of people over the building of organizations, knowing that when they take care of the part, the whole will be healthy. Failing to develop the part, the whole stands less of a chance of being productive over the long haul. Keeping that in the forefront of your thinking and planning becomes a challenge; the natural leader part of you will want to elevate the organization over the individual.

Matching people to roles according to their gifts is essential. The purpose of an organization is to maximize the strengths of people and minimize their weaknesses. By harnessing the abilities and talents of people, you'll create a synergistic effect. An effective leader is a matchmaker who marries people and roles. There are no wrong people, just wrong positions. The leader's job is to help people succeed. The best chance of this is by placing them in positions that unleash their talents. Don't worry about working on a weakness, unless it sabotages a strength.

Mere aptitude tests can fall short in unveiling strengths. Here is a brief list of organizational quotients to assess and observe:

IQ (Intelligence Quotient): Spiritual leaders sometimes underestimate the role of IQ. This is pretty much a God-given factor. It does not reflect education, but rather a capacity to process information. Put low-IQ people in demanding situations and you'll overwhelm them, stressing them out and frustrating others. Place people with higher IQs in simple roles and you'll bore them to death.

AQ (Attitude Quotient): Attitude is contagious, so make sure you place high-AQ people in places where they can infect others with their positive energy. Low-AQ people are negative, pessimistic, and melancholy in nature, so try to keep them away from where their attitudes will adversely affect other people and decision making.

RQ (Resource Quotient): First analyze the type of resources a person has: time, talent, or treasure. Especially in volunteer organizations, time and treasure factors become as big as talent issues. People who have talents but limited time must be used strategically. People with treasures but little time can provide needed capital to fund projects.

PQ (People Quotient): High-PQ people are good relationally. They shine among others. Place these people in front-end customer service roles. They'll make your organization appear better than it is. Low-PQ people are good behind the scenes, where they won't bore, offend, or alienate others. Use their other gifts, but keep them out of public or team-leading venues.

MQ (Maturity Quotient): Emotional and spiritual maturity provide great stability within people. Decision makers, mentors, and influencers need a certain level of consistency, insight, and discernment. Talented people lacking maturity are attractive, but they can be organizational kindling, starting unnecessary fires and making messes.

EQ (Energy Quotient): There are turtles and there are rabbits. You can't do a lot about energy levels. Don't overwhelm turtles or you'll lose them. Conversely, let the rabbits run, but put measures in place to ensure accuracy and completeness. Provide them with plenty of things to do and don't team them up with turtles and therefore frustrate them. High EQs can handle a lot on their plates and thrive on busyness.

CQ (Commitment Quotient): CQ is the key to unlock the other quotients. The greatest frustration for any leader is to have people with high quotients who lack motivation and commitment. Low-CQ people will hold back, while high-CQ people will go the extra mile. One of the primary tasks of spiritual leaders is to raise the level of commitment among followers and potential followers.

Once you've assessed a person's quotients, matching the person to the role becomes the final task. The better you are at matching strengths with organizational needs, the more effective you will be. If people flounder in the roles you've assigned them, assume first that *you've* failed.

The most effective leaders:

1. Know the strengths of their people
2. Match these strengths with organizational roles
3. Don't worry about weaknesses (unless they deplete the strengths)

HOW DO SPIRITUAL LEADERS DEVELOP NEW LEADERS?

There are three types of leaders: The first are people who have few leader aptitudes, but who find themselves in leader roles for various reasons. Many hardworking, smart, and managerial people get elevated to positions they're not designed to fulfill. They need to study leadership as a process and work through the influence abilities of others. Second, there are leaders who are naturally gifted at getting teams together, motivating, and developing people. And finally, some leaders are those who develop other leaders. Leaders are different from followers, so developing leaders around you becomes a significantly different process from developing followers, requiring unique skills and strategies.

So, how do you raise up and develop leaders with varying degrees of influence ability and work through them for the benefit of the organization? Leaders who fail to raise up other leaders stunt the growth of an organization, as well as risk their own health due to stress.

First, learn to recognize people with leading capacity. Who do people turn to for answers? Who naturally develops followers? Who has exhibited leadership in past experiences? Not everyone has the capacities to influence others. Sometimes troublemakers are influencers who merely need mentoring and positive unleashing. Leaders rarely flock. You will have to handpick them, one at a time.

Second, take the time to invest yourself in them. Seek them out and challenge them to be discipled. Jesus put most of his efforts into the Twelve rather than into the masses because he had limited time but much at stake. Focus on honing skills and maturity where it is needed. Spiritual leaders may need to work more on developing spirituality than on their leading skills. Young leaders may require more mentoring than motivating. Each person is unique. One size doesn't fit all.

Third, train them on the job. Give them small tasks to fulfill, to see how they respond. Nothing reveals leading capacity better than challenging it to action. Were they overwhelmed? Did they offend people? Were they successful? If not, why? If so, then give them another task to accomplish with a team, but this time a little larger or more important one.

Finally, unleash them into significant areas of influence. After overseeing ten and then fifty, let them oversee a hundred and then a thousand. By putting more of your time and energy into leader development, you increase your influence exponentially.

When leaders are unwilling to share power and limelight, they run the risk of limiting an organization's potential. The most effective organizations are veritable leader factories, raising up and developing those with varying influence capacities within their ranks. Most organizations recruit leadership talent from outside the organization, which is often a sign that a previous leader didn't develop leaders from within.

How Do Spiritual Leaders Care for the Spiritual Side of Their Followers?

Because leaders are in the people business, they do well to understand how people function. Just as a farmer understands the characteristics of both the soils and the crops, a leader must know his or her people. This includes the spiritual aspect of a person, for in that individual's soul is the core of all he or she is—relationships, career, dreams, hobbies, health, and family. When leaders don't recognize the influence of the soul on all aspects of the person, they fail to understand how to motivate, empower, and develop their most valuable assets: people. Organizational pimping is where you use people for their knowledge and skills, with little respect to their value created in the image of God. Recognizing this God-image in leading is a primary characteristic of spiritual leadership.

Spiritual leading is more complex than non-spiritual in that it considers the entirety of a person. Most work situations overlap physical and intellectual aspects. But when people discover their passion and mission in life, this emanates from the soul. The reason for so much job dissatisfaction and career malaise is that we tend to segregate spirituality from our work, creating an energy shortage and inability to revitalize ourselves.

People who tap their souls for work and other activities experience a self-renewing benefit. They're able to expend large amounts of energy without burnout and destructive stress, while at the same time harvesting satisfaction and contentment from what they do. External observation makes you think these people are content because they are effective, but closer analysis would show you that their productivity is more a result of being fulfilled in the process of living their dreams.

The ability to see into the soul of a person is an important part of developing the individual. A healthy soul is much more apt to be a productive member of the team than someone with a sick spirit. Every spiritual leader is also a spiritual doctor. Whether you're trained to be a pastor or called to priestly duty is immaterial. You must nurture the souls of those you lead if you're to fulfill the responsibilities of a spiritual leader.

Pray for people. Offer to pray with them about personal and professional matters. Every organization will be different in terms of what you can and can't do. Employees of overtly non-spiritual corporations realize that it's difficult to determine the boundary of what can and can't be done in terms of spiritual development. But most spiritual leaders will discover that they can significantly impact the lives of those within their spheres of influence, vertically as well as horizontally. When we are in tune with our souls, we are aware of others' souls.

HOW DO SPIRITUAL LEADERS CREATE A CULTURE THAT NURTURES THE SOUL?

A leader is the caretaker of corporate culture. A spiritual leader is the CSO—chief spiritual officer. Spiritual leaders are responsible for nurturing an environment that is at best a place to grow spiritually and at least a place where people will not be prone to soul damage. If you're the spiritual leader of an organization, you must decide early whether you want to develop a nursery or a mortuary. Even churches can be detrimental to spirituality and businesses routinely drain the soul. But it doesn't need to be this way. Organizations reflect people. Leaders have the ability to establish polity, choose priorities, and create reward systems. When soul-depleting practices prevail, a spiritual leader's job is to take a stand, using his or her influence to squash anti-spiritual practices.

Over time, an organization tends to reflect the soul of the leader. There's no such thing as a Christian organization, only an organization with Christians in it. When spiritual leaders adequately prepare their own souls, those associated with them will experience the fruit. A leader cannot *not* influence according to his or her values, beliefs, and practices. The more a leader is in tune with the Creator, the greater the impact the Spirit will make on the organization.

Leaders who are spiritual, but not spiritual leaders, segregate their souls from work and corporate culture. People know them as good people, but very little of their spirituality shows up in their leading. Spiritual leaders, on the other hand, know that they can't separate true spirituality from what they do. They've been entrusted with a divine duty not only to achieve organizational goals, but also to harness and care for the spiritual condition of the people they employ and who employ them. Every person is at a different place in his or her pilgrimage with God. You can't treat everyone alike. Work should enhance spiritual growth, not deter it.

Leaders are teachers. They can stack the deck during training, motivational meetings, and communication pieces. They can set priorities and discuss major and minor themes, depending on what's appropriate. Being a spiritual leader at work is not the same as being a Bible thumper or pushy evangelist. Subtle yet assertive reliance on Scripture, biblical principles, and people skills will influence those you lead. If policy allows, pray in meetings. If not, develop healthy relationships that allow pre- or post-work conversations around spiritual themes as a viable alternative to using company time for overt soul growth.

You can also use stories as a means to incarnate values. To express specific values, talk about an employee or team member who took a moral and relational stand in the course of work. Returning overcharged money, firing a dishonest employee, deciding to keep the stores closed on Sunday to allow people time for family worship, team building, and relationship nurturing are all ways of elevating spiritual values, even in "non-spiritual" organizations.

Spiritual leaders observe the emotional climate within organizations, understanding that emotions often reflect the boundary between the intellect and the soul. Change either cognitive or spiritual conditions and you'll affect the emotions. Outside of chemical imbalances, our spiritual and mental processes pretty much determine our emotional state. Physical influence is tertiary (being healthy, rested, ill, tired, and so on). So by rewarding the presence of spiritual fruit (love, joy, peace, and so on), a leader can positively create an atmosphere that encourages soul growth.

Look out for spirit killers—people who distract others from God and moral values. Weed sowers abound in society, and when organizations bring people together, you're bound to have a few who influence others negatively. Keep an eye on those who intimidate soul growth within teammates. Don't allow the vulnerable to be forced to work under such an influence. Do your best to recruit people who exude a healthy, spiritual approach to life.

WHAT DO RELATIONSHIPS IN AN ORGANIZATION HAVE TO DO WITH SPIRITUAL LEADERSHIP?

Natural leaders tend to vary in their people skills, but the very function of leaders practically mandates that they be in roles where relationships will be strained. Difficult decisions, limited time with people needing attention, confronting aberrant behavior and attitudes, jealousy, not to mention the ongoing misperceptions people have about you simply because you're in a role of influence and limelight—all can result in relational tensions. Leaders with inadequate people skills sometimes use these conditions as a convenient camouflage. Unfortunately, this becomes a justifying, self-deceiving, blind spot that prevents leaders from becoming more effective in their relationships. Wise and humble leaders understand when an inordinate amount of their relational friction is self-induced.

Aside from normal relationship strains, one sign of low spiritual energy is tension or alienation from people who are close to the leader—team members, superiors, family members, friends, and church associates. One or two sideways relationships don't necessarily reflect a trend, but more than that often does. Strained relations include finding yourself irritated by or angry at people who interact with you. These attitudes and behaviors emerge during conversations, phone calls, and meetings. Alienated relations have more to do with people who are aloof because of unaddressed tensions, unforgiven hurts, and general avoidance. While emergency flares rarely warn leaders that a problem exists, astute leaders will consider the possible reasons behind relational coolness.

As you study the Bible, you'll discover a direct, positive correlation in relations with people above and below you organizationally. True spirituality will significantly affect your inter-actions with others. It's difficult to be in tune with God and out of sync with other people.

> With the tongue we praise our Lord and Father, and with it we curse men, who have been made in God's likeness. Out of the same mouth come praise and curs-ing. My brothers, this should not be. Can both fresh water and salt water flow from the same spring? (James 3:9-11)

Enemies vary in number and degree according to the situ-ation (remember, even Jesus had enemies), but when rela-tions of people closest to the leader are strained, this is a sign of spiritual dryness. If we're creating sparks with those who know us and love us most, we need to consider what may be happening within us. The primary indicator of spiritual presence is love:

> If I speak in the tongues of men and of angels, but have not love, I am only a resounding gong or a clanging cymbal. If I have the gift of prophecy and can fathom all mysteries and all knowledge, and if I have a faith that can move mountains, but have not love, I am noth-ing. (1 Corinthians 13:1-2)

Therefore, we shouldn't be surprised that spiritual fortitude results in valuable people skills, often referred to as spiritual fruit.

WHAT ARE SOME INDICATORS OF SPIRITUAL LEADING FOUND IN RELATIONSHIPS AND ATTITUDES?

Perhaps the greatest indicators of true spiritual leadership are found in a series of responses referred to as spiritual fruit.

But the fruit of the Spirit is love, joy, peace, patience, kindness, goodness, faithfulness, gentleness and self-control. . . . Those who belong to Christ Jesus have crucified the sinful nature with its passions and desires. Since we live by the Spirit, let us keep in step with the Spirit. (Galatians 5:22-25)

What does the fruit of the Spirit have to do with leadership? The list of spiritual fruit is the DNA of the Holy Spirit. When God's Spirit is present, leadership is characterized by these elements. When leadership is not spiritual, these factors are consistently missing or inadequately present, making them difficult to find. Following is a fruit list in the context of spiritual leadership.

Do you express adequate love? Why do people follow leaders? The reasons vary from person to person and situation to situation. But the strongest emotion is love. When people respect you as a leader, they'll follow you up to a point. But when followers both respect and love a leader, they'll climb mountains with him or her. Love usually reciprocates itself. Human love usually loves because of or in response to what it receives. When you see people as pawns to be used within an organization or as sources of hassles to be avoided, they'll resent you. When they resent you personally, it's always more difficult to lead effectively. And in non-crisis situations, it's often impossible. Do you love the people you lead? Do you know who they are? Do you communicate care, concern, and compassion? These are vital to effective leading, because leading is nothing more and nothing less than a unique relationship with people. If people don't sense love from you as a leader, they'll withdraw some amount of influence from you.

Do you reflect a joyful attitude? "Happiness" is a word based around happenings or circumstances. But what happens when circumstances become dismal and negative? Happiness flees. Joy has to do with an inner disposition toward hope. When hope is high, you can be joyful, regardless of any pain. Leaders are influencers. People need hope in order to follow. When you're low on joy, you deplete the hope and positive attitudes among your followers. You may not say anything, but people can usually tell the state of mind of their leader. Most often, your job is to keep your fears to yourself and share your encouragement. When leading becomes a hassle or when you start to lose your personal joy, as well as an ability to exude joy to your team and organization, you lose effectiveness.

Do you exude sufficient peace? It's been said, "Peace is joy at rest; joy is peace dancing." Leaders who emote peace aren't easily frazzled. They convey hope and confidence to their people. As we've discussed, a leader wears various hats in his or her role, one of which is that of an organizational parent. Children look to their parents for security and direction. When a parent is insecure and fearful, this creates insecurity and fear within the children. When Mom or Dad is stressed and tense, the whole family takes on that emotional state.

An important role in leading is exuding peace to the organization, even in times of stress and vulnerability. The Bible is full of peace and fear-not passages. Demonstrating peace expresses an attitude that says, regardless of circumstances, we can still make it. When we're relying on God in our lives, peace is present most of the time. When our fear and lack of peace make us irritable, negative, critical, and defensive, these are signs that we're ebbing in spiritual fervor and strength.

Do you maintain effective patience? Few leaders can claim patience as a natural strength. They're creatures of change and action. Many people think they are being patient when they are really just procrastinating, are reticent to act, or are covering up fear or a lack of direction. Savvy leaders don't confuse disregard with patience. Healthy patience is the realization that in spite of all we do, God is God and does things in his time.

A lack of patience creates stress among team members and diminishes their long-term productivity and current enjoyment, often shortening their tenure. Impatient leaders tend to make decisions that are detrimental to long-term effectiveness by striving to pick fruit before it's ripe. The old saying, "I don't have ulcers; I give them," is a trademark of the non-spiritual leader. The patient spiritual leader must act with speed at times, but pushing people without concern for their well-being is a sign of human leading. Impatience is a symptom of feeling out of control, that things are not working as planned, and even incompetence. ("I'm frustrated I can't figure this out so I'll push even harder.") Impatience is a sign of being spirit-low.

Do you respond to people with kindness? Congeniality, being personable, and professional politeness are very important characteristics in effective leading. Think of at least one leader you know who lacks kindness in his or her demeanor toward others. Barking commands and being moody, rude, and short-tempered are all signs of the Spirit's absence. Spiritual leaders respond favorably to people. People respond well to spiritual leaders who express kindness.

Poise, etiquette, and being mannerly often separate a great leader from a merely good one. Two leaders may accomplish the same goal, but the one who is kind will probably dominate. There's rarely a reason not to be kind while leading, regardless of the situation. People need to know your heart. If you're kind, they'll perceive you as a good leader—one others want to follow. If you're mean-spirited, cool, aloof, and seemingly disinterested in the mundane issues of others around you, it could indicate a lack of spirituality. Jesus took time for children and to heal a lame man on his way. People frequently interrupted his travels. When you're kind only if things are going well or kind only toward those who stand the chance of helping you, you're communicating human power, not God's.

Do you consistently express goodness? Goodness refers to moral conditioning, character, and ethical integrity. If you cut corners on a sale, deal with people underhandedly, or ask your followers to look the other way about something, you're demonstrating a lack of spirit. Moral excellence is a natural fruit of God's presence in our lives. Holiness shows itself best in leadership, because we're so tempted to compromise at times in order to achieve.

Life seems to be less black-and-white in the twenty-first century. The problem with dabbling in hues of gray is that we justify our lack of spiritual spine, finding it easier to compromise for a win. Group and organizational achievement may appear paramount, but achievement at all costs results in prostituting ourselves and others. We lose our souls, even if we gain the whole world. When we misplace our moral compass, when our motives come into question on more than one occasion, and when we start to cut corners regarding ethics and standards, these are signs that we're working out of human energy.

Are you faithful toward God and followers? While faithfulness is often seen as an attitude of a leader toward the task at hand, it is actually relational, because collaborators look for this trait in the leader. Perseverance both in leading and in commitment to God are the essence of faithfulness. When we are tempted to give up before it's time because we lack vision or the hope that things will change, this is a sign that our spiritual life may be waning. Tenacity, stick-to-itiveness, and purveying a sense of hope are vital to effective leading. People look to leaders for faith. They rarely commit to a project when a leader lacks it. When you have a difficult time conveying hope, fail to muster a sense of positive expectations, or don't believe in the people you're working with, consider your spiritual energy level. Giving up is not always wrong, but when you feel a desire to quit, first check the level of your spiritual fuel tank.

Are you gentle in your demeanor? Twenty-first-century leading is far kinder and more gentle than the more industrial, twentieth-century version. Top down, autocratic, male-dominated, authoritarian leading is not a sign of spiritual leading. Coercion is about being a bully, not a leader. Manipulation, emotional game playing, and threats are all means of human leading.

The velvet-covered brick approach—being strong on the inside but soft on the outside—allows you to be gentle with people while not being weak or soft. In cultures where men and women are educated and experienced and people have multiple involvement options, there's little tolerance for rough leadership. When you find yourself relying on force, power, authority (position), and verbal manipulation, it's a good sign that you may have lost your spiritual fortitude. When you have power, you don't have to flaunt it. When you don't have it, you'll strive to influence people via harsh means.

Do you have adequate self-control? When you find yourself wandering, overeating, working endless hours, and perhaps being tempted sexually or by drugs, alcohol, or materialism, you have good reason to believe you're lagging spiritually. A common misunderstanding is that you need self-discipline in order to be more gentle, loving, patient, and so on. For example, the thinking goes: "If I had self-control, I wouldn't lose my temper or run off at the mouth." But according to this spiritual teaching, self-control is more of a by-product rather than a prerequisite of spiritual fervor. Usually, a lack of self-control expresses itself according to our innate weaknesses. A leader may be weak at holding his or her tongue, or keeping sexuality in check, or saying "no" to opportunities that dilute his or her potency where it's needed. When we see wrong behavior popping up in our lives, it's a sign that we're lagging in spiritual energy.

You've probably never thought of a leader as a fruit farmer, but if you're going to be a spiritual leader, you need to become one. Every farmer knows that the formula for a great harvest is inherent in every healthy seed. The farmer's responsibility isn't to grow the fruit. That will come naturally. His or her job is to create as many good conditions as possible to let the seed do what it is preprogrammed to do. Matching seed with soil type, climate, and the calendar is important. Fertilization, irrigation, cultivation, and similar processes are vital.

Spiritually speaking, the leader who wants to be spiritual needs to understand that high-quality people skills are an innate part of God's Spirit that can be allowed to grow in us. Our job is to provide a fertile, receptive, cultivated environment where that seed can flourish. Far too many Christians strive to emanate the fruit of the Spirit under human energy. "What other way is there?! You mean to tell me I don't have to try to be more loving, joyful, peaceful, or patient?" That's correct. You're off the hook with regard to producing fruit. You're not off the hook in terms of providing an inviting environment where that seed can flourish. The difference is a matter of process and product. God will grow the spiritual seed in you if you just give him the right environment.

> *"I am the true vine, and my Father is the gardener. . . .*
> *Remain in me, and I will remain in you. No branch can*
> *bear fruit by itself; it must remain in the vine. Neither*
> *can you bear fruit unless you remain in me.*
>
> *"I am the vine; you are the branches. If a man remains*
> *in me and I in him, he will bear much fruit; apart from*
> *me you can do nothing. If anyone does not remain in me,*
> *he is like a branch that is thrown away and withers; such*
> *branches are picked up, thrown into the fire and burned.*
> *If you remain in me and my words remain in you, ask*
> *whatever you wish, and it will be given you. This is to*
> *my Father's glory, that you bear much fruit, showing*
> *yourselves to be my disciples." (John 15:1-8)*

Be good soil. That's what abiding is all about. Make sure you present yourself to God every day as good dirt, available garden space. He'll grow the seed.

WHAT HAPPENS WHEN A SPIRITUAL LEADER FAILS?

One of the first things you learn in the martial arts is how to fall without getting hurt. Teaching how to fall doesn't promote the idea of falling. Rather, it recognizes that falling is possible and that the welfare of the body is at stake if you don't fall well. Leaders who create accountability structures usually avoid falling. But if they do fall, they should humbly submit to the appropriate people for correction and rehabilitation. The organizational recovery plan should be appropriate for the failure—not too much, not too little. Board members must step forward to lovingly reprove. Too many organizations shoot their wounded instead of helping them heal. Team members should be kept informed to avoid misinformation (gossip). They should convey thanks for all the good the leader has done, while recognizing that failure must not be overlooked. But rarely does failure need to be fatal or final.

When a leader fails, others in roles of influence must share the blame by asking these questions: "Where did we fail? Did we put too much pressure on the leader or overlook the stress? Did we select the leader poorly? How did we miss the early symptoms of falling? Why did we not provide suitable accountability?" Certainly, leaders can fall anyway, but many do so needlessly when their organizations fail to care for their success. Far too many organizations treat the fallen leader as an enemy, denying any participation in his or her downfall. This is usually a case of denial.

Leaders who fall need to humbly submit to their superiors or accountability board. Those holding the leader accountable must perform triage to assess the damage to the organization. The concern is for the organization first, the leader second. If the offense makes it seem necessary to reject the leader, the leader should move on voluntarily, for the sake of the organization. Leaders can't deny the importance of culture. Losing trust and respect within a culture reduces the influence of a leader, rendering him or her impotent. Position is meaningless without power.

Once the accountability entity assesses the damage and assigns an appropriate discipline, some sort of restoration process is appropriate. If the leader isn't rejected by the organization, a comeback plan is needed, including timeline conditions, recovery assignments, and behavior expectations. The plan may include professional counseling, time off, tighter accountability, and gradual reestablishment in responsibilities. Establishing a contract or clearly communicating the process is important. Staff, board members, and others will need to handle responsibilities during the restoration process.

If the leader is rejected by the organization, a restoration process should still take place for potential future leading. Good leaders may be imperfect, but they're hard to come by. Salvaging them through a strong but grace-giving restoration process also provides hope to others who may not want to get into a leader role because they are afraid of failing.

There are few clear biblical guidelines for dealing with leaders who experience moral and spiritual failure. Every restoration plan needs to be custom-designed. The fact that organizations are people working together means they are bigger than the leaders themselves. Those involved are also partially responsible for the good and bad decisions of the leader. Usually, those ready to cast the first stone are guilty in some dark region of their own lives. No one wins when a leader falls, but reducing the damage is what a good restoration plan seeks to provide.

WHAT HAPPENS WHEN THE GOAL OR THE ORGANIZATION FAILS?

There is no such thing as a 1.000 batting average for a leader. Success can't be measured in terms of always accomplishing organizational goals, but one measure is the leader's effectiveness in catalyzing people toward a goal. In other words, the goal of the leader is different from the goal of the organization. You can't always determine the success of the leader based on the success of the organization. When a group doesn't accomplish a goal, the leader's job is to thank the members and encourage them, even if the leader feels defeated. The most difficult thing to remember when goals are inadequately accomplished is that this may have little to do with leading and leadership. We've stated this several times, but it's important here: The goal of a leader is to catalyze the process by which people work together toward common objectives. Of course, the hope is that accomplishing organizational objectives is a by-product of the process. But true leadership is measured in terms of maximizing teamwork within the given circumstances and resources.

If leaders are only successful when they accomplish organizational goals, then we'd have to chalk up Moses as a marginal leader for not getting the people of Israel into Canaan. David failed for not being able to build the Temple. Spiritual leaders recognize that true success is measured in terms of potential and the fulfillment of God's will. "My food," said Jesus, "is to do the will of him who sent me and to finish his work" (John 4:34). Spiritual maturity comes in recognizing we all have the same destiny in life: to do God's will. What that looks like will be different from person to person and even seasonally over the course of a life. Spiritual leaders realize that while they may appear to fail miserably from a human perspective, they may be valiant winners in divine terms.

Measuring success as a spiritual leader is difficult. What matters most is not where you are, but from where you've come. Who you've developed matters more than what you've accomplished. What it took to get where you are matters more than how far you've traveled. That's why comparisons can be so deceiving and ultimately demotivating. Human leaders compare, compete, and think themselves superior if they're ahead of others. Spiritual leaders compare who they are with who they believe their Creator has called them to be. Ultimately, only your Maker can determine how effective you are as a leader, even though perceived success will greatly enhance your ability to influence others down the road.

Of course, people who use this concept of success as justification for never accomplishing anything probably have a leading problem, either in being unable to recognize achievable goals or impotent to catalyze a team effectively. The phrase "God calls us to be faithful, not successful" sounds good, but those who quote it frequently tend to use it like a "Get Out Of Jail Free" card. Mature leaders avoid such responses.

Regardless of real and perceived failure, spiritual leaders do their best to respond to circumstances honestly and with courage, focusing on the concerns of others. Typical corporate leading these days seems to be more about packing your own golden parachute in case you need to bail if the company goes down. Huge compensation packages and dismissal fees may reflect shrewd personal economics, but spiritual leaders look beyond their own feelings and needs, and they work to minister to team members. When an organization fails to accomplish its goals, feelings of failure, disappointment, and disunity quickly emerge. "Going down with the ship" may be an antiquated rule, but the leader's job is to make sure everyone else is in a life boat before fleeing for personal safety.

Again, failure doesn't need to be fatal. Nearly all great leaders undergo various times of personal and professional failure. Spiritual leaders allow these times of brokenness to tenderize their souls and remind them of their dependence on the sovereign God. By being broken in the right place—the soul— spiritual leaders turn failure into fertilizer for future character fruit. By providing a greater capacity for God, spiritual leaders guide their team members through periods of defeat with the long view in mind.

[Solomon said,] "Now, LORD God, let your promise to my father David be confirmed, for you have made me king over a people who are as numerous as the dust of the earth. Give me wisdom and knowledge, that I may lead this people, for who is able to govern this great people of yours?"

God said to Solomon, "Since this is your heart's desire and you have not asked for wealth, riches or honor, nor for the death of your enemies, and since you have not asked for a long life but for wisdom and knowledge to govern my people over whom I have made you king, therefore wisdom and knowledge will be given you." (2 Chronicles 1:9-12)

SECTION 7

A Spiritual
Leader's Skills

How does a spiritual leader handle conflict
without damaging souls?

How does a spiritual leader set the emotional climate of a group?

How and when does a spiritual leader share a negative concern?

How should a spiritual leader respond to criticism?

How far should spiritual leaders go in compromising?

How does a spiritual leader handle betrayal?

How can spiritual leaders be sure they're leading with vision?

How can spiritual leaders leave honorably?

HOW DOES A SPIRITUAL LEADER HANDLE CONFLICT WITHOUT DAMAGING SOULS?

If you can't stand the heat, get out of the kitchen. If you can't create some heat, get out of the kitchen. Leaders must become comfortable in dealing with friction and sparks, because they are public figures, because they pursue change and innovation, and because it's their job to settle disagreements. If you enjoy conflict, you need therapy. But running from it destroys your ability to lead. Mishandling conflict causes more damage within organizations than the issue behind the conflict. As you've learned, spiritual leaders go about this process differently than non-spiritual ones. They express greater concern for the well-being of people and relationships, and they strive to emanate godly characteristics of grace and compassion.

First, don't fear conflict. It can be your friend if it raises issues that are circumventing progress. Conflict is often an expression of anger, which is an emotional phase of most change sequences. It can mean that people are processing the new idea. People who fear conflict usually aren't leaders. They're managers, nurturers, peacekeepers, and maintainers.

Second, don't jump to conclusions that those in conflict against you are enemies. People rarely get involved in things they don't care about. Leaders know that commitment is an important ingredient of leadership, even if it gets turned sideways from time to time. Viewing others as opponents establishes an adversarial atmosphere, where you reject the other person instead of segregating the issue at hand from the relationship. Pursuing a win/win outcome or at least saving face for the person in conflict is significant. Rising above the emotions without appearing insensitive is a precarious balance to maintain.

Third, respond appropriately. While there is no need to take out a mosquito with a bazooka, it's also inappropriate to put a Band-Aid on a gaping wound. Perhaps the best blueprint for handling conflict was explained by Jesus:

> "If your brother sins against you, go and show him his fault, just between the two of you. If he listens to you, you have won your brother over. But if he will not listen, take one or two others along, so that 'every matter may be established by the testimony of two or three witnesses.' If he refuses to listen to them, tell it to the church; and if he refuses to listen even to the church, treat him as you would a pagan." (Matthew 18:15-17)

Here are some basic conflict guidelines:

- If the issue doesn't matter, let it go. Chalk it up as flack generated by trivial conversations, gossip, innuendo, self-expression, opinions, and shop talk. If you try to iron out every wrinkle, you'll waste precious energy. Take note but remain silent.

- If the issue seems serious or if it entails an influencer, deal with it on a personal level, face to face, gathering facts and gaining perspective. As a leader, assume your duty of initiating contact. Realize that nine times out of ten, people will not initiate conversation with you. Refuse the temptation to write confrontational notes or e-mails. They nearly always worsen the situation. Contentious people are often influencers needing information, discipleship, or attention.

- If resolution doesn't take place between you and the person with a conflict, bring in another person who might serve as a witness and a third perspective. Accountability and feedback are appropriate to avoid game playing and to provide support.

- If the conflict is still not resolved, bring in others who can work out an appropriate decision as a team. A wise leader will listen to these views, without deferring responsibility for the decision to be made.

- Finally, if someone is at odds with leadership, that person should be asked to leave as a member of the team, yet continue to be loved as an outsider. The good of the organization is of paramount importance. Allowing division to deplete valuable energy is unacceptable. At the same time, premature dismissal can reduce momentum and repel potentially strong allies.

Unfortunately, there's no such thing as conflict malpractice insurance. Spiritual leaders have the upper hand because, if they're relying on spiritual means, they have three things they need in large quantities during conflict. All of these emanate from God's Spirit.

First, the Spirit supplies grace and compassion so that people feel loved, attended to, and are not alienated too soon. Second, he provides peace, so that the leader remains levelheaded, gaining his or her identity from God rather than solely from the support and affirmation of others. Finally, the Spirit gives suprahuman wisdom. According to James 1:5, "If any of you lacks wisdom, he should ask God, who gives generously to all without finding fault, and it will be given to him." Conflict is like fire. It can light a path or burn those who mishandle it.

HOW DOES A SPIRITUAL LEADER SET THE EMOTIONAL CLIMATE OF A GROUP?

The primary goal is to keep your attitude faithful and full of hope. As a spiritual leader, your attitude will affect others naturally through your mere presence and influence. Therefore, maintaining the demeanor of your soul becomes paramount. Spending time alone with God, grooming the garden of your soul so that it blooms flowers instead of growing thistles, is essential. But because you're a human, prone to the full range of emotions, what do you do with the potentially poisonous "plants," like anger, loneliness, doubts, and fear? These have the ability to poison your organization, making messes that require time and energy to correct.

The Psalms give us the spiritual solution. Throughout the 150 psalms and prayers of this Old Testament hymnal are some pretty heated passages that find little attention in most church services. They're full of anger, hate, hurt, and a sense of gloom and loneliness. Imagine a congregational responsive reading with these verses: "O Daughter of Babylon, doomed to destruction, happy is he who repays you for what you have done to us—he who seizes your infants and dashes them against the rocks" (Psalm 137:8-9). But if you'd seen your babies and your friends' toddlers beaten to death by foreign soldiers invading your home, you'd feel the same way. The beauty in passages like these is that they are given to God. Leaders err when they use their groups as therapy sessions for their own discomforts. The temptation to vent in front of those we lead is common, but practicing this is self-sabotage. An unhealthy alternative is to suppress the anger so that it emerges through high blood pressure and depression.

Admit your feelings of anger, despair, and fear, but confess them primarily to God. Tell him. He can handle your dumps far easier than people can. When you honestly, openly share your negative emotions with God, he sanctifies them and they lose much or all of their poisonous potency. Human wisdom would suggest, "Oh just suck it up. Hold it in. You're the leader." But instead of corking these emotions and letting them manifest as ulcers and heart disease, spiritual wisdom says to take them to your Boss, the Leader of all leaders, the Creator of the universe—God.

David, one of the greatest leaders, who also happened to be a musician, wrote many of the psalms as leader therapy. Moses commonly went before God with his complaints about the stubborn people he was leading. Even Jesus sneaked away from the disciples and masses to spend time in prayer. In the Garden of Gethsemane, he was honest with God about his desire to avoid the pending challenge, even though he never fully shared that concern with those he was leading.

Another example of spiritual wisdom is seen in the life of Job, recorded in the oldest book in the Bible. After he underwent incredibly adverse circumstances, losing his children, wealth, health, and even the support of his wife, Job did not "sin with his mouth," in what he said. He didn't let his prevailing emotions dictate his words. Job is the epitome of human maturity: the ability to exude faith and commitment to God regardless of circumstances. As James tell us,

> We all stumble in many ways. If anyone is never at
> fault in what he says, is a perfect [leader], able to keep

*his whole body in check. . . . Likewise the tongue is a
small part of the body, but it makes great boasts.
Consider what a great forest is set on fire by a small
spark. The tongue also is a fire, a world of evil among
the parts of the body. It corrupts the whole person, sets
the whole course of his life on fire, and is itself set on
fire by hell. (James 3:2,5-6)*

Our words are indicators of our soul's condition. What we
say reveals what's inside. The words of leaders are attitude
cues for others. When a leader talks, people listen—and then
they repeat, discuss, and react, positively or negatively.

HOW AND WHEN DOES A SPIRITUAL LEADER SHARE A NEGATIVE CONCERN?

Leaders endanger an organization when they don't appropriately warn people of pending danger. The key is strategy.
Henny-Penny-sky-is-falling hand wringing invokes undue
stress and too much of it desensitizes the team when real danger is lurking. But because most people are change-averse by
nature, preparing the climate for improvement usually
requires selling the problem before the solution. Often a fine
line exists between being negative and being bluntly honest.
Negativity leaves followers with despair; honesty leaves them
with a burden, but also with hope.

Honesty is always the best policy. Openness is not necessarily the best policy. Discerning the difference is an attribute
of leading. Until people understand the need for change, they
won't be interested in the remedy. Raising the level of pain can
be necessary both on an individual basis and organization-
wide. Weak-kneed leaders who are unwilling to hurt the
patient with a needle prick are willing to let the patient die of
some more serious disease.

The key isn't so much what's said but how it's said. "I perceive that you might be more effective in a different role." "Our growth trends aren't what we like to see. We're not living up to our potential." "Let's talk about how you can help us be more effective." Leaders must estimate the potential outcome of the terminology and body language they use. The challenge of any communication is that people often don't hear what we think we're saying or communicating. People tend to fill in the blanks and usually with negative conclusions. Be honest, be fair, but leave them with hope. Rarely will a true spiritual leader not garnish the bad news with some sort of optimistic outcome or positive possibility. The leader who leads by fear is usually replaced as soon as it's convenient.

Napoleon said, "Leaders are dealers in hope." The word "gospel" means "good news." Someone said, before you share the good news, you need to be good news. Enthusiasm is contagious. As has been popularly taught, the Greek word for enthusiasm (en theos) means "in God," "God in me." Smiles, warm greetings, friendly gestures, energetic welcomes, positive lessons, optimistic e-mails, thank-you notes, and public vision statements are all ways of turning up the thermostat within a team or organization. Seize opportunities to pat a back, high-five a team member, or shoulder hug a new customer. A few degrees of temperature change, up or down, can create a comfort zone where people can enjoy serving in your leadership.

HOW SHOULD A SPIRITUAL LEADER RESPOND TO CRITICISM?

One beauty aid for an attractive soul ironically comes from a strange source—criticism. Like dung fertilizing a garden, a critique, investigation, or public review can actually grow the fruit within the heart of a spiritual leader that's only available through such trials. Many people fail to confront leaders appropriately because they feel intimidated or powerless or feel that their suggestions will go unheard, or worse, that they'll be labeled a troublemaker and be ostracized within the organization. Thus, most resort to gossip, armchair coaching, or underground "discussions." Value and reward those who confront you appropriately, regardless of the substance of their critique.

Spiritual leaders may be more vulnerable than others to being hurt by critique, because their primary motivation is to serve God and others, not to gain power, money, or fame. They assume people know their hearts, and therefore they may feel confused and misunderstood when people criticize them. Regardless of your motives, know that leading and being critiqued are kissing cousins.

Not much is written about receiving criticism, other than the idea of sucking it up and accepting it as a burden to bear as a leader. Here are some quick ideas on handling this hot potato with dignity. Some leaders are better than others at receiving critical comments, whether those comments are a personal critique of your role as a public figure or a professional assessment of an idea or method you're advocating. Regardless, you can learn a few disarming devices and grow from the common pain of critique.

Recognize that criticism has more value to a spiritual leader than to others, because it has the power of keeping the leader humble. Spiritual people know how vital humility is to maturity and spiritual growth. Spiritual leaders understand their dangerous role of dealing in the realms of power and notoriety, which can create pride, a toxin to the soul.

Make note of who is giving the criticism. Is he or she a friend or a foe? What's the history of this person with the organization? Naysayers are a dime a dozen and have little to lose in sharing a negative comment. Pay attention to trends, but consider random comments from habitual pessimists as junk mail. If, on the other hand, a loyal staff member, influencer, or confidant shares a concern or critique, listen.

Think about what's being said. Is the critique about an idea, a personal behavior or attitude, or a concern about a fellow team member? Is the matter one of perception, of communication/information, or of substance? Perceptions are real and important in leadership. Each of these aspects imparts a different response. Don't jump to conclusions that substance needs defending until you've considered communication and perception.

Look at how the criticism is being expressed. Is the person in a good spiritual state or out of the Spirit? Discernment is important here. Reading people's nonverbal cues is just as vital as listening to their words. Most find it difficult to lie with their body language. Is the person in a terrible place personally and transferring these negative emotions? Is the person legitimately concerned, desiring to help you and the organization succeed? Was it a face-to-face meeting or an anonymous note, blind e-mail, or grapevine-behind-the-back sort of message requiring you to initiate an inquiry?

Avoid a defensive mode. This can be very difficult to do, especially when you haven't set the agenda and the criticizer hasn't taken the time to prepare you for the confrontation. But when you're in a defensive mode, you appear insecure and have a difficult time actually hearing valid concerns and motives. Assume that most people are poor at communicating negative news. They'll do a crummy job of caring for your feelings, sticking to the issue at hand, and confronting you privately and in the Spirit. Forgive them in advance for their style, but listen to the critique without drawing conclusions. At this point, perception is often more important than the substance of the conversation. Make sure people feel listened to and that you're open to hearing new ideas, regardless of the quality of their comments.

Thank the critic after listening, dialoguing, and unpacking suggestions. If possible, respond, "Let me think about these things." This may be a legitimate desire to ponder the thoughts and seek friendly counsel as to the validity of the criticisms. Or it may be a plea for time to cool down and pray before you say something you'll regret. In either case, it's certainly a sincere and loving way of making sure the person feels listened to.

Criticism comes to you as a leader because you affect followers' lives. You have the power and responsibility to serve others. You're a public figure, a community resource. It's both a blessing and a curse. Criticism isn't an exception; it's the norm. The key to responding well to criticism—from friends or foes—is remembering that as a spiritual leader you're ultimately serving God, not people or yourself.

> *Whatever you do, work at it with all your heart, as working for the Lord, not for [people].* (Colossians 3:23)

Your goal isn't to make everyone happy or to impress people with your leading skills, but to fulfill the will of your Creator. Play to an audience of One.

Brokenness via critique is a vehicle for keeping the spiritual leader sensitive, dependent upon God, and reliant on divine sustenance. They're both tough and tender, developing resilient hides that cover sensitive hearts. As a result of criticism, spiritual leaders learn to identify with the down-and-outer, the ostracized, and the ridiculed.

HOW FAR SHOULD SPIRITUAL LEADERS GO IN COMPROMISING?

Pressure-cooker situations create circumstances where spiritual leaders must reach inside themselves and discern the Spirit's leading. A self-righteous ideology to never compromise is naïve at this point. But a spiritual leader must walk the fine line between accomplishing good with mild compromise and losing what could be accomplished with absolutely no compromise. Jesus said to spiritual leaders, "I am sending you out like sheep among wolves. Therefore be as shrewd as snakes and as innocent as doves" (Matthew 10:16).

Spiritual leaders in the twenty-first century must at times be willing to compromise on minor issues so that they're able to succeed with major ones. Compromise doesn't mean negating the Ten Commandments or denying Christ. It does mean being shrewd and even risking being misunderstood by uncompromising followers who aren't aware of the complexities involved in a situation. Unfortunately, no single biblical template serves as a guide. Historical leaders such as Joseph, Daniel, Meshach, Shadrach, and Abednego didn't seem to budge an inch amidst conflicting foreign values and high stakes. Yet Nehemiah negotiated time and resources to rebuild Jerusalem's walls. God himself occasionally "compromised" initial opinions when leaders such as Moses pleaded the case for his people. David dealt shrewdly with his enemies in order to live with the Philistines while being chased by King Saul. Queen Esther negotiated a deal for her people at just the right time. Compromise is a practice of politics, and politics is nothing more or less than people being in relationship with each other.

Jesus was a compromiser in the way he dealt with the adulterous woman, sinners, and in performing miracles and eating on the Sabbath. He seemed to commend even drastic negotiation when it made sense.

> "The master commended the dishonest manager because he had acted shrewdly. For the people of this world are more shrewd in dealing with their own kind than are the people of the light." (Luke 16:8)

Obviously, Peter compromised too much when he denied Jesus on the night of the betrayal. Not becoming putty in the hands of ungodly people is the theme of Romans 12:1-2. Knowing what to fight over and where to draw the line is the stuff of spiritual leadership, where spiritual wisdom and power are essential.

Ideological purism is a convenience of less complex times. For the higher good to prevail, leaders can't go to war like legalists. Unfortunately, godly compromisers are apt to be attacked from both ends of the spectrum. The bigger issue of compromise comes in the question, "Am I doing this to keep peace or am I doing this because it's the right thing to do?" Non-leaders compromise in order to avoid conflict and make people happy. The goal of saving one's own face usually results in avoiding truth. Happiness is a pleasant convenience when it happens, but it's rarely a priority in spiritual leading.

Wishy-washy leaders are chameleon-like, changing colors to match the popular vote and current environment. People lacking a clear, strong value system become spineless spin artists, forever looking to popularity polls for their guidance instead of to a higher truth. On the other hand, purists rarely accomplish much in this day. They may be prophetic, but prophets rarely lead well, resorting to hermit-like behaviors in the desert. Martyrs are needed occasionally, but in greater demand are leaders who'll wrestle with the messiness of conflicting interests. Spiritual leaders have the advantage in complex times because they possess a strong inner value system. Spiritual leaders also benefit from spiritual power that enables them to make decisions that may not be popular from either or both sides of the matter.

The issue of compromise is *what's* right rather than *who's* right. Seeking seasoned, wise people is a valuable tool for spiritual leaders. Young leaders often rely too heavily on their own natural skills and too little on the wisdom of sage elders. Answers are often found in asking the right questions. Some of these might be:

• Is this a personal issue that I'm making public, merely because I'm the leader?

- What do I stand to lose by not giving in at all? And what do I stand to gain?
- Am I willing to lose my job for this issue? Is this a wise decision, to risk failure over such a concern?
- Do I have a more significant issue pending in the near future, for which a compromise now might gain needed power resources?
- Will I be able to sleep at night if I compromise on this matter?
- *What is God's will? Have I paid the price to discover it?*

How Does a Spiritual Leader Handle Betrayal?

What do you do when people say things behind your back and work to undermine your leading? Is a spiritual leader insulated from the pain of treason? Does he or she respond with forgiveness, only to be trampled by a power-seeking follower or position-hungry influencer? Nothing tests the character of a leader like betrayal. Spiritual leaders are neither vengeful nor milk toast. They keep the big picture in mind and understand that even the best of people are at times attacked from behind.

If you never trust people, you'll never be a leader, because leaders must empower others and delegate authority. While you can reduce blind spots and maintain effective feedback channels as a pre-strike warning system, you must also take risks with people and organizationally. Don't confuse smart leading with cynicism and paranoia. Don't kick yourself when betrayal happens: *I should have seen it coming. Shame on me for putting my faith in them.* Some of the finest spiritual leaders have been crucified and stabbed in the back, even by close friends and family.

One way to reduce the pain of feeling betrayed is to look at the motives of those who are working against you. Do they sincerely believe they are doing what is best for the organization or are they seeking personal gain? Do the people know what they are doing or do they merely lack adequate information? Are your betrayers being truly subversive or is the stress of leading causing you to be paranoid and overly sensitive? Leaders must stand up to those who seek to undermine an organization from within. Organizational arsonists must be stopped. Power embezzlers rob precious resources. Double spies need to be confronted. Leaders must consider what's best for the organization. Spiritual leaders are best equipped to surrender pride and ego and respond with personal sacrifice and forgiveness.

Perhaps the biggest challenge after being betrayed is to trust again. Spiritual leaders must comply with the command to forgive, again and again, just as any Christ-follower does. Spiritual leaders leave revenge to God, not to lawyers. They seek to be blameless, not to win at all costs.

How Can Spiritual Leaders Be Sure They're Leading with Vision?

While many leadership books discuss vision, we can't near the end of our discussion about leading without at least mentioning it. Needless to say, vision has everything to do with leading, and it has special meaning for spiritual leaders.

A vision is a leader's mental image that conveys where an organization needs to be in the future. It primarily addresses the what, why, and when. "How" follows. Vision is primarily right-brained and passionate. It evokes emotions. A result of vision is setting goals and developing strategy. It doesn't work the other way around.

For a vision to be authentic, we can't feel fulfilled staying where we are for long. Four characteristics determine the quality of a vision: clarity, urgency, importance, and size. If any of these arenas is inadequate, you diminish the intensity of your vision and lessen the effect it has on your followers.

time" (Ecclesiastes 3:11). Knowing the proper timing is certainly more of an art than a science.

There are two concepts of time in ancient Greek language, one referring to quantity and one to quality. Counting time is a Western civilization obsession. Calendars, stopwatches, and work deadlines dictate our lives, but ironically, these structures can reduce our fruitfulness. We think more in terms of how much time something will require, instead of basing strategic plans on readiness or ripeness. Eastern cultures focus more on proper timing. This is the meaning behind Solomon's wisdom, "in its time." Farmers know that effective harvesting is done when the crop is ripe and ready, not when the gestation date pops up on their Outlook calendar or Palm Pilot planner. Leaders are organizational farmers. They must discern when strategic decisions need to be made, including their departure.

When a leader leaves prematurely, ugly things happen. A good leader makes sure suitable infrastructure is in place and managerial systems are functioning before departure. An often overlooked aspect in newer organizations is having a confident, competent process outlined for selecting the next leader. When those left behind don't know how to replace the leader, they're apt to make a bad and hurried hire, adversely affecting the organization. When leaders chase new opportunities or leave behind messes, they're behaving irresponsibly.

The weakness in most leaders, as in most followers, is to leave prematurely. Some fruit only happens after significant time. Leaders seeking bluer skies are often their own worst enemies when they keep uprooting themselves, not to mention their families. They never experience the unique reward of long-term labor. Some of us aren't wired for longevity, but the weakness of a majority of leaders is leaving too soon. Stick it out through tough times. Take a sabbatical if you feel burned out. Don't make significant decisions when you're depressed or overly tired.

When a leader stays too long, ugly things happen as well. Transcending your time of effectiveness is akin to relatives who overstay their welcome. You love them, but you aren't quite sure how to ask them to leave. Entrepreneurs who don't change leading styles, leaders who've not implemented an innovation in years, and those who've grown the organization beyond their capacity to lead are destined to do harm. You mean well, but your failure to recognize when you've outlived your effectiveness is a very difficult thing, shrouded by denial.

Listen for cues from trusted influencers. Look honestly at productivity statistics. The theory that a leader shouldn't leave in the middle of projects is inadequate, because any healthy organization will always be midstream in various projects. Sometimes, a project can be so draining that the organization needs new leadership energy to finish it. Be honest with yourself and the fruits of recent labor.

Spiritual leaders consider what's best for the organization. Waiting around until a certain retirement age may result in a lame duck administration. Letting the organization languish while pursuing personal or other professional objectives is selfish. The organization doesn't exist for your benefit. You exist within the organization for its benefit. While we all hope for a win/win situation, the health of the organization takes precedence. When the organization would benefit more from your departure than from your staying, it's time to leave. Obviously, these are subjective estimates, because you don't know how it will fare with your staying or leaving. Seeking wise counsel is often challenging as well, because a conversation with anyone within the organization can create anxiety, speculation, and gossip. Seeking counsel outside the organization can also be limiting, because these people aren't attuned to what may be best for the organization.

Spiritual leaders rely primarily on spiritual cues for their discernment, far more than on circumstantial or even personal feelings.

*Since we live by the Spirit, let us keep in step with the
Spirit. (Galatians 5:25)*

Keeping cadence with the Spirit is vital for leaders, not only
as they lead, but also as they leave, because their influence
impacts so many. Losing touch with the Spirit is like a drum
major who is out of sync with the beat of the song. His or her
leading messes up the entire marching band. Preparing for
your departure is important. If polity allows, take sufficient
time to develop a successor, and when you pass the baton, do
it fully. Exiting leaders can do much to pave the way for those
who follow them, enhancing the chances of a healthy transition. Lingering in the shadows can hamstring the new leader's
effectiveness.

When you do depart, applaud those who have helped you.
Thank everyone for allowing you the opportunity to serve
them. Don't review sour grapes, make apologies, or linger in
regrets. Celebrate! Accept kudos as gifts—deserved or unde-
served. Encourage people left behind that their true compass
is God and that in times of transition, as always, we must ultimately rely on him. Leaving in dignity is the final touch of
leaving a legacy.

Spiritual leaders realize that they are but ordinary people
who've been blessed with a unique opportunity to help people
accomplish together what they couldn't do alone. Finally, they
humbly thank God for his guidance, power, leading, and love,
without which they wouldn't be spiritual leaders at all.

A Spiritual Leader's Commitment

The discussion of spiritual leading could fill volumes. The array of topics and characteristics expressed in this book are but a sampling of the possibilities. More than likely, I've missed some important aspects that you'd like to have addressed.

The goal of this book is to nurture a certain way of thinking, an attitude toward using your gift of leadership in a way that transcends mere human talent. Within the realm of spirituality is the best place to make sure that you accomplish this powerful role most effectively and responsibly, serving people and ultimately bringing glory to God. Everyone benefits when leaders lead boldly and under the guidance and power of the Spirit.

Spiritual leaders must be spiritual first, leaders second. Human nature and the demeanor of leading mean that if leadership is the first priority, spirituality will be a very distant second. Such leading will lack spiritual potency. More than any time in history, this century calls for men and women who will courageously endeavor to be strong, diligent spiritual leaders.

Spiritual Leader Manifesto

I will endeavor to submit my talents, intellect, energies, and will to God. I don't exist to fulfill my own pleasures or ambitions.

I'm a servant, and I use leadership as my primary tool for serving. My calling is to pursue godly goals. My model is Christ. My mission is to boldly catalyze change for the good. My goal is to emulate love and faith so as to create hope and to help those within my span of influence reach their potential.

About the Author

Alan E. Nelson is the author of books such as *Embracing Brokenness* (NavPress), *My Own Worst Enemy*, *Leading Your Ministry*, *The Five Star Church*, *The Five Secrets of Becoming a Leader,* and *How To Change Your Church.* He is a columnist for *Rev.* magazine and *Leadership Wired,* and a speaker/trainer for organizations such as Willow Creek Association, Group, and Leadership Training Network. He has a doctorate in leadership from the University of San Diego. His other degrees are in biblical literature and psychology/communication.

Alan is the founder and senior pastor of Scottsdale Family Church in Arizona. He and his wife, Nancy, have three sons. Alan can be reached at alann@scottsdalefamilychurch.org.

HELPFUL BOOKS FOR GROWING IN CHRIST.

Embracing Brokenness

Pain, struggles, and suffering—we can *go* through them or *grow* through them. Learn how a godly view of brokenness brings purpose and meaning to life's inevitable disappointments.
(Alan E. Nelson)

Christian Coaching

Coaching is a hot topic today. Dr. Gary R. Collins shows us how to combine the successful principles of coaching with a God-centered application to help others realize their maximum potential.
(Gary R. Collins)

The Mentored Life

This book introduces you to a framework for discipleship and helps you gain a greater understanding of God's desire to mentor us.
(James A. Houston)